W9-CRR-742

Nature Guide to
Yosemite National Park

Yosemite National Park: the Basics

History and Facts

Established: October 1, 1890

Visitors: 4,200,000

Designations: World Heritage Site, 1984; Globally Important Bird Area

Natural Historic Landmarks: 5—Wawona Hotel and Thomas Hill Studio, LeConte Memorial Lodge, Parsons Memorial Lodge, Rangers' Club, the Ahwahnee Hotel

National Register of Historic Places: 60 properties, including Yosemite Valley Chapel, Tioga Pass Entrance Station, Wawona Covered Bridge, Camp Curry Historic District, Vogelsang High Sierra Camp Historic District, Mariposa Grove Historic District

National Scenic Trail: Pacific Crest National Scenic Trail

State: California

Time zone: Pacific Standard Time (PST)

Official park website: nps.gov/yose

Physical Features

Acreage: 759,210, including 704,624 acres of designated wilderness

Elevation: Lowest point: 2,127' at Merced River; highest point: 13,114' at Mount Lyell

Peaks above 13,000': 3

Waterfalls: 9 above 317', including Yosemite Falls at 2,425' (tallest in North America)

Water resources: Lakes: 318; rivers and streams: 880 miles

Average annual precipitation: 37.2" (Yosemite Valley)

Temperature range (F): 28°F to 89°F (10 to 20 degrees cooler at higher elevations)

Plant species: 1,500 species of flowering plants, including 35 trees (18 conifers) plus shrubs, grasses, sedges; plus 26 ferns, 11 fern allies, 500+ lichens, 300+ fungi

Animal species: About 150+ birds; 90 mammals, including one federally endangered species (Sierra Nevada bighorn sheep); 6 native fish; 22 reptiles; 12 amphibians, including one federally endangered frog; 110+ butterflies; well over 300+ invertebrates

Wildlife population estimates: 250 to 500 black bears; 40 to 50 mountain lions

Facilities

Entrance stations: 5—*South:* South Entrance via CA 41; *West:* Arch Rock Entrance via CA 140; *East* (summer to late fall): Tioga Pass Entrance via CA 120; *Northwest:* Big Oak Flat Entrance via CA 120; *Northwest:* Hetch Hetchy via CA 120/Evergreen Road

Visitor centers: 3—Yosemite Valley Visitor Center, Wawona Visitor Center at Hill's Studio, Tuolumne Meadows Visitor Center

Roads: 214 miles paved roads; 68 miles unpaved roads; 20 miles paved walks and bicycle paths

Tunnels: 5

Trails: 800 miles of trails, including 70 miles of the Pacific Crest National Scenic Trail that overlap portions of the John Muir Trail

Campgrounds: 1,504 total sites: *Yosemite Valley:* Upper Pines, 238; Lower Pines, 60; North Pines 81; Camp 4, 35; *South of Yosemite Valley:* Wawona, 93; Bridalveil Creek, 110; *North of Yosemite Valley:* Hodgdon Meadow, 105; Crane Flat, 166; Tamarack Flat, 52; White Wolf, 74; Yosemite Creek, 75; Porcupine Flat, 52; Tuolumne Meadows, 304

Picnic areas: *Yosemite Valley:* Cathedral Beach, Sentinel Beach, Swinging Bridge, Church Bowl, Lower Yosemite Fall, El Capitan; *South of Yosemite Valley:* Wawona, Mariposa Grove Road; Glacier Point; *North of Yosemite Valley:* Yosemite Creek, Tenaya Lake, Lembert Dome

Lodging: *Yosemite Valley:* The Ahwahnee, 123 units; Yosemite Lodge, 245 units; Curry Village, 498 units; Housekeeping Camp, 24 units; *South of Yosemite Valley:* Wawona Hotel, 104 units; *North of Yosemite Valley:* Tuolumne Lodge, 69 units; White Wolf, 28 units; High Sierra Camps, 55 units

Food: *Yosemite Valley:* Yosemite Village: Degnan's Loft, Delicatessen and Cafe, Village Grill; The Ahwahnee: Ahwahnee Dining Room, Ahwahnee Breakfast Bar, The Ahwahnee Bar; Yosemite Lodge: Food Court, Mountain Room Lounge, Mountain Room Restaurant; Curry Village: Coffee Corner / Ice Cream, Curry Village Bar, Pavilion, Pizza Deck, Meadow Grill Happy Isles Snack Stand; *South of Yosemite Valley:* Wawona Hotel Dining Room, Glacier Point Snack Stand; *North of Yosemite Valley:* Tuolumne Meadows Grill, Tuolumne Meadows Lodge Dining Room, White Wolf Lodge

Fuel: *Yosemite Valley:* none; *South of Yosemite Valley:* Wawona Gas Station; *North of Yosemite Valley:* Crane Flat, Tuolumne Meadows

Nature Guide to Yosemite National Park

Ann and Rob Simpson

FALCONGUIDES

GUILFORD, CONNECTICUT
HELENA, MONTANA

AN IMPRINT OF ROWMAN & LITTLEFIELD

FALCONGUIDES®

FalconGuides is an imprint of Rowman & Littlefield.
Falcon, FalconGuides, and Outfit Your Mind are registered trademarks of
Rowman & Littlefield.

Distributed by NATIONAL BOOK NETWORK

Map revised by Alena Joy Pearce. Original map provided by the National
Park Service.

British Library Cataloging-in-Publication Data is available on file.

Library of Congress Cataloging-in-Publication Data is available on file.

ISBN 978-0-7627-8161-4 (paperback)

∞™ The paper used in this publication meets the minimum
requirements of American National Standard for Information
Sciences—Permanence of Paper for Printed Library Materials,
ANSI/NISO Z39.48-1992.

Contents

YOSEMITE NATIONAL PARK

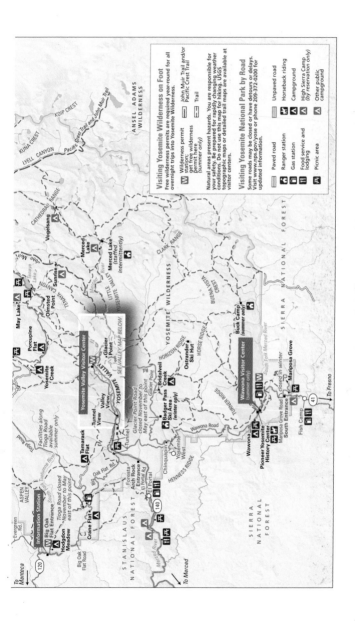

Visiting Yosemite Wilderness on Foot

Free wilderness permits are required year-round for all overnight trips into Yosemite Wilderness.

W Wilderness permit station; get free wilderness permit here (summer only)

John Muir Trail and/or Pacific Crest Trail

Trail

Natural areas present hazards. You are responsible for your safety. Be prepared for rapidly changing weather conditions. Do not use this map for hiking. USGS topographic maps or detailed trail maps are available at visitor centers.

Visiting Yosemite National Park by Road

Some roads may be closed or have detours or delays. Visit www.nps.gov/yose or phone 209-372-0200 for updated information.

Paved road

Unpaved road

Ranger station

Horseback riding

Gas station

Campground

Food service and lodging

High Sierra Camp (by reservation only)

Picnic area

Other public campground

To Manteca

120

ASPEN VALLEY

STANISLAUS NATIONAL FOREST

Evergreen Rd

Hodgdon Meadow

W Information Station

Big Oak Flat Entrance

Big Oak Flat Rd

Crane Flat

Tioga Road closed November to May east of this point

South Fork Tuolumne River

Tamarack Flat

Facilities along Tioga Road available summer only

Tioga Rd

Yosemite Creek

May Lake

Olmsted Point

Tenaya Canyon

Porcupine Flat

Yosemite Creek

John Muir Tr

CATHEDRAL RANGE

ANSEL ADAMS WILDERNESS

KOIP CREST

Pacific Crest Trail and John Muir Trail

KUNA CREST

LYELL CANYON

Vogelsang

Merced Lake (staffed intermittently)

Merced Lake

Sunrise

TENAYA CANYON

LITTLE YOSEMITE VALLEY

Merced River

YOSEMITE WILDERNESS

CLARK RANGE

Glacier Point

SEE VALLEY MAP BELOW

YOSEMITE VALLEY

HORIZON RIDGE

Ostrander Ski Hut

Bridalveil Creek

BUENA VISTA CREST

Buck Camp (summer only)

W

HORSE RIDGE

SIERRA NATIONAL FOREST

Tunnel View

Valley View

Glacier Point Road closed November to May east of this point

Glacier Point Rd

Badger Pass Ski Area (winter only)

Tunnel

Yosemite West

El Portal Rd

Big Oak Flat Rd

Forestal Arch Rock Entrance

El Portal

140

Chinquapin

HENNESS RIDGE

Wawona Road

TURNER RIDGE

Wawona

Pioneer Yosemite History Center

W

Wawona Visitor Center (summer only)

Mariposa Grove

Mariposa Grove Road closed in winter

South Entrance

Fish Camp

41

To Fresno

Merced River

South Fork Merced River

SIERRA NATIONAL FOREST

Merced River

To Merced

YOSEMITE VALLEY VISITOR CENTER

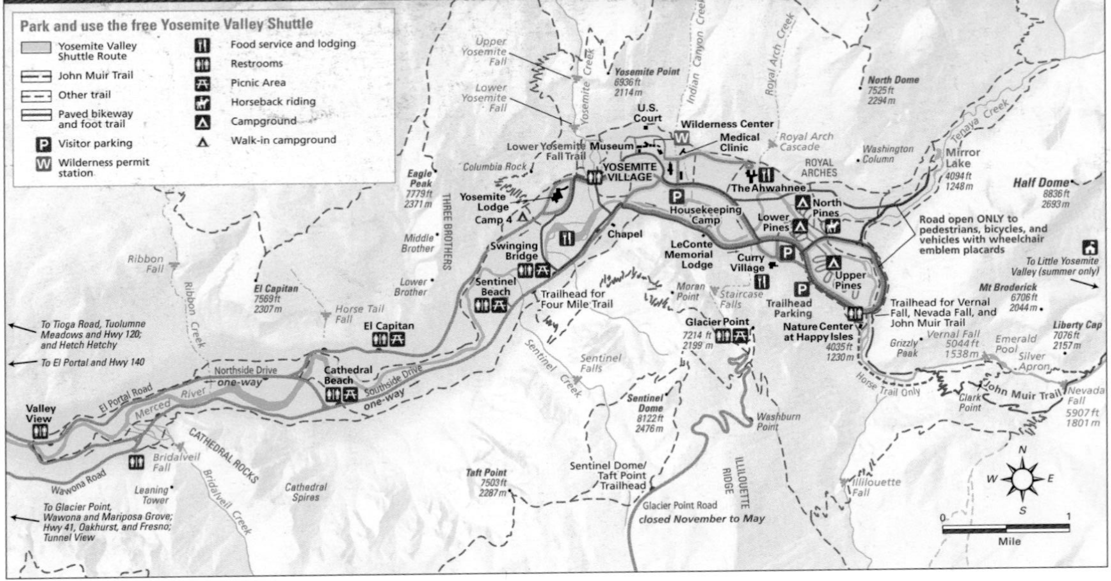

Acknowledgments

Many thanks to the superb park personnel and volunteers of Yosemite National Park, who have dedicated their lives to preserving the natural resources of the park and sharing its natural wonders with visitors. We would especially like to thank Sarah Stock for sharing her wealth of knowledge about the park's natural history. Others who have provided insight or contributed in other ways to this book are Michael Elshon Ross, David Lukas, Alison Colwell, Joe Medley, Greg Stock, Tom Medema, Erik Westerlund, Judy Womack, Kylie Chappell, Christine White Loberg, Lisa Thompson, Mary Kline, and Paul Ollig. Our thanks also to Belinda Lantz and the staff and members of the Yosemite Conservancy for their continued support of the interpretative and educational mission of the park. We would also like to thank all the staff at FalconGuides and Globe Pequot Press, whose support and efforts made this National Park Nature Guide series a reality. We especially thank our son James for his work on processing the images for this and previous books in this series. We would like to dedicate this book to our family, who have supported us with encouragement and understanding during the research, writing, and photography of this nature guide.

To the reader, we hope this guide helps open your eyes to the wonders of nature and, in doing so, generates a spark of love for the plants and animals that rely on us for their continued existence in important natural habitats such as those in Yosemite National Park.

Falling 2,425 feet in three stages, Yosemite Falls is the seventh-tallest waterfall in the world.

About Yosemite Conservancy

Millions of park visitors experience the work of the Yosemite Conservancy every year, whether hiking a restored trail, standing at a beautiful overlook, spotting protected wildlife, earning a Junior Ranger badge, or joining an Outdoor Adventures program. Through the support of donors, Yosemite Conservancy provides grants and support to Yosemite National Park to help preserve and protect Yosemite today and for future generations. The Conservancy is dedicated to enhancing the visitor experience and providing a deeper connection to the park through outdoor programs, volunteering, and wilderness services. Thanks to dedicated supporters, the Conservancy has provided more than $81 million in grants to Yosemite National Park. Learn more at yosemiteconservancy.org, or call (800) 469-7275.

Year-round birding opportunities in Yosemite include Yosemite Conservancy programs and the annual Christmas Bird Count.

Introduction

The *Nature Guide to Yosemite National Park* is an easy-to-use, pocket-size field guide to help visitors identify some of the most common plants, animals, and natural features of the park. Technical terms have been kept to a minimum, and color pictures accompany the descriptions. Perfectly sized to fit easily into a daypack, this compact field guide is filled with interesting information about each organism, including natural history and ethnobotanical notes and other historical remarks. We care for the things that we know. Intended as an introduction to nature in Yosemite National Park, this small book will hopefully spark an interest in the natural world and generate further interest in caring for and supporting the environment. You can refer to the "References" section at the end of this book for more information and resources for in-depth identification purposes.

Scientists in Yosemite provide important research information about park wildlife and resources.

About Yosemite National Park

A natural wonder, Yosemite National Park is known worldwide as a destination of magnificent beauty. About four million visitors come here each year with the expectation of seeing a great wonder, and yet their first sight of Yosemite Valley often brings an unexpected emotional response. The awe-inspiring granite cliffs, thundering waterfalls, craggy peaks, and luxurious emerald meadows that inspired John Muir in his campaigns of conservation still captivate visitors today. The breadth of beauty here runs deeper than the granite cliffs. At the foot of Half Dome, the enduring drama of life exists in the tiniest flower to the regal eagles that soar over their valley.

American Indians of this area, such as the Miwok and Paiute, understood that apart from the scenic beauty, these valleys and mountains held abundant natural resources that sustained them. They studied and learned about the behavior of animals as well as the secrets of the forests and how to distinguish one plant from another, and they learned to listen silently to the ebb and flow of nature. In Yosemite Valley, the Yosemite Museum offers a fascinating look into the cultural history and use of natural resources.

Visitors soon agree that Yosemite (pronounced "Yo-SEM-it-tee") is a park of significant diversity and magnificence. Declared a World Heritage Site in 1984, the park protects a wide array of plants and animals, some of which are endangered or threatened, such as the Sierra Nevada bighorn sheep and the great gray owl. New to science, the Yosemite cave pseudoscorpion (*Parobisium yosemite*) is a tiny arachnid that gained status as a species in 2010. Some plants, including the Yosemite orchid, have their origins within park boundaries.

The park offers ranger-led programs that help educate visitors about the many wonders of Yosemite. In Yosemite Valley, the Nature Center at Happy Isles is a good place to learn about the natural processes that shaped the valley. Classes are offered through the Yosemite Conservancy throughout the year, highlighting nature from birds to wildflowers to geology. Check the Conservancy website for more in-depth nature books, such as *Sierra Nevada Natural History* by Storer, Usinger, and Lukas. In an easy-to-read format, *Geology Underfoot in Yosemite National Park* by Glazner and Stock will help you understand the complex geological processes that have shaped this area.

It is highly recommended that you begin your visit with a stop at one of the visitor centers, where you can pick up a park map and learn about activities such as the Junior Ranger program and other events. There is an entrance fee for Yosemite National Park; see the park website (www.nps.gov/yose) for current fees. The America the Beautiful—National Parks and Federal Recreational Lands Annual Pass is available, as is the Senior Pass for US citizens and permanent residents age 62 or older. Permanently disabled citizens are eligible for a free Access Pass; active duty military members and dependents are eligible for a free annual pass.

Although the park is open daily, some visitor services are closed from October to April. Tioga Road and Mariposa Grove Road are generally closed in winter. You can check road closures by calling the park information line at (209) 372-0200 or check the park website at www.nps.gov/yose. Transportation to the park is available through the Yosemite Area Regional Transportation System, or YARTS (877-989-2787; yarts.com). The Yosemite Valley Shuttle System is highly recommended for transportation in Yosemite Valley; best of all, it's free. Check at the visitor center or one of the lodges, campgrounds, or other facilities for a current schedule and map. Information on seasonal transportation, lodging, camping, and activities is also available in the official park newsletter, Yosemite Guide, available online at www.nps.gov/yose.

Check the park website for food and lodging availability in the park. Lodging reservations are available at yosemitepark.com or (801) 559-5000. During the peak visitor season (June through August), the lodges and campgrounds fill early and advance planning is necessary. Food, lodging, fuel, and other services are also available at the towns bordering the park. See "Common Destinations in or near Yosemite National Park" for help with planning your visit. The Yosemite Conservancy provides carefully selected educational materials to park bookstores to enrich your visit. Two of the Conservancy's publications that will help you plan your visit are Steven Medley's *Guidebook to Yosemite* and the *Road Guide to Yosemite* by Bob Roney, both available on the Conservancy website and in park bookstores. Please consider joining the Conservancy's efforts to support the much-needed efforts of park personnel (yosemiteconservancy.org).

Common Destinations in or near Yosemite National Park

Many visitor services in Yosemite National Park are open year-round. You can check the Yosemite Guide for current opening and closing times at www.nps.gov/yose. Reservations for some campgrounds in the park are available at recreation.gov or (877) 444-6777; all other campgrounds are on a first-come, first-served basis. For current campground availability, call (209) 372-0266. Fuel and other services are also available at towns bordering the park; please note that there may be lengthy distances between fuel stops and plan accordingly. Restrooms are located at visitor centers and at most picnic areas. Due to winding roads and relatively slow speed limits, driving time in Yosemite is typically longer than anticipated for the mileage indicated (see "Driving Times" in the introduction). Roads into Yosemite are normally open 24 hours a day, but severe weather or other emergencies may necessitate closure at any time. Tire chains or cables are required to be in your possession when entering a designated chain control area from October through April, or as posted. For more information visit the Yosemite National Park website at www.nps.gov/yose. For current road status in the park, call (209) 372-0200 (press 1, then 1). For road conditions outside the park, check the California Department of Transportation (Caltrans) website at dot.ca.gov or call (800) 427-7623. (*Note:* cell phones do not work in many areas of the park.)

Services in Yosemite

Gas Stations (24-hour self-serve) (none in Yosemite Valley)
Wawona
Crane Flat
El Portal
Tuolumne Meadows (summer)

Garages
Village Garage (24-hour towing): (209) 372-4637

Lodging—Reservations: (801) 559-5000; yosemitepark.com
Yosemite Lodge at the Falls (Yosemite Valley)
Ahwahnee (Yosemite Valley)
Curry Village (Yosemite Valley)
Housekeeping Camp (Yosemite Valley)
Wawona Hotel (Wawona)
White Wolf (Tioga Road; summer only)
Tuolumne Meadows (Tioga Road; summer only)
Yosemite West (private inholding) various private owners and companies; yosemitewest.com
The Redwoods (private inholding): (877) 753-8566; redwoods inyosemite.com

Camping—Campground reservations: (877) 444-6777; www .recreation.gov
Yosemite Valley—Upper Pines, Lower Pines, North Pines, Camp 4
South of Yosemite Valley—Wawona, Bridalveil Creek
North of Yosemite Valley—Hodgdon Meadow, Crane Flat, Tamarack Flat, White Wolf, Yosemite Creek, Porcupine Flat, Tuolumne Meadows

Visitor Centers / Information plus Books and Field Guides
Valley Visitor Center
Wawona Visitor Center at Hill's Studio (seasonal)
Tuolumne Meadows Visitor Center (seasonal)

Tour Reservations
Tour desks at Yosemite Lodge, Yosemite Village, Curry Village, and The Ahwahnee; (209) 372-1240

Horse or mule rides: (209) 372-8348

Bicycle rental: Yosemite Lodge, Curry Village •

Food Service
Yosemite Village
Yosemite Lodge area
The Ahwahnee
Curry Village
Wawona
White Wolf (summer)
Tuolumne Meadows (summer)

Groceries / Camp Supplies
Village Store (largest grocery store in Yosemite)
Yosemite Village
Yosemite Lodge
Curry Village
Wawona Store
Crane Flat
Tuolumne Store (summer)

Showers / Laundry
Curry Village Showers
Housekeeping Camp Laundromat

Medical / Dental Services
Yosemite Medical Clinic: (209) 372-4637
Dental Services: (209) 372-4200 or (209) 372-4637

Internet Kiosks
Degnan's Deli
Yosemite Lodge Lobby

Photography Supplies and Classes
The Ansel Adams Gallery: (209) 372-4413; www.anseladams.com

Outdoor Activities, Programs, Classes
Wilderness Center, Yosemite Valley: (209) 372-0740; www.nps
.gov/yose/planyourvisit/wpres.htm—for wilderness permits
and to rent bear canisters

Tuolumne Meadows, at shuttle stop #3 on road to Tuolumne
     Meadows Lodge
Yosemite Mountaineering School (YMS)—Rock climbing
     classes and hikes: (209) 372-8344
Tuolumne Mountaineering School and Stables: (209) 372-8435
NatureBridge—Youth programs: (209) 379-9511; yni.org
Yosemite Conservancy: (800) 469-7275; (415) 434-0745—
     Outdoor Adventure Programs; (209) 379-2317; yosemite
     conservancy.org

Gateway Towns
South: South Entrance via CA 41
     Oakhurst: lodging, food, fuel
West: Arch Rock Entrance via CA 140
     El Portal: lodging, food, fuel
     Mariposa: lodging, food, fuel
Northwest: Big Oak Flat Entrance via CA 120
     Groveland: lodging, food, fuel
     Merced: lodging, food, fuel, hospital, all services
East: Tioga Pass Entrance via CA 120 (summer to late fall)
     Lee Vining: lodging, food, fuel

Black Bear

Driving Times (Approximate)

From	To	Approximate Time
South Entrance	Yosemite Valley	1 hr., 15 min.
South Entrance	Mariposa Grove	5–10 min.
South Entrance	Wawona	5–10 min.
Wawona	Yosemite Valley	1 hr.
Glacier Point	Yosemite Valley	1 hr.
El Portal	Yosemite Valley	30 min.
Big Oak Flat Entrance	Yosemite Valley	1 hr.
Yosemite Valley	Crane Flat	30 min.
Yosemite Valley	Hetch Hetchy	1 hr., 30 min.
Yosemite Valley	Tenaya Lake	1 hr., 15 min.
Yosemite Valley	Tuolumne Meadows	1 hr., 30 min.
Yosemite Valley	Tioga Pass	1 hr., 45 min.
Mariposa	Yosemite Valley	1 hr., 15 min.
Groveland	Yosemite Valley	1 hr., 30 min.
Oakhurst	Yosemite Valley	1 hr., 30 min.
Fresno	Yosemite Valley	2 hr., 30 min.
Merced	Yosemite Valley	1 hr., 30 min.
San Francisco	Yosemite Valley	4 hr., 30 min.
Sacramento	Yosemite Valley	4 hr.
Stockton	Yosemite Valley	2 hr., 30 min.
Modesto	Yosemite Valley	2 hr., 10 min.
Mammoth Lakes	Yosemite Valley	2 hr., 30 min.
Lee Vining	Yosemite Valley	2 hr., 10 min.
Sequoia & Kings Canyon National Parks	Yosemite Valley	3 hr., 30 min.

Elevations of Common Park Sites

Destination	Elevation (feet)
Badger Pass Ski Area	7,200–7,800
Clouds Rest	9,926
Crane Flat Campground	6,200
El Capitan	7,569
El Portal	1,939
Glacier Point	7,214
Half Dome	8,842
Hetch Hetchy	3,800
Hodgdon Meadow Campground	4,900
Mariposa Grove	6,000
Mount Dana	13,057
Mount Lyell	13,114
Tenaya Lake	8,149
Tioga Pass Entrance Station	9,945
Tuolumne Meadows	8,575
Wawona	4,000
White Wolf Campground	8,000
Yosemite Valley	4,000

Safety Notes

Roads through Yosemite are uniquely designed to afford motorists with spectacular views. The maximum speed limit is generally 45 miles per hour, but in some areas it drops to 25 miles per hour or less. There are some steep grades and winding, tight curves, some with very little sight distances. Use caution when you are passing by or pulling out of one of the turnouts along the road. Perhaps the greatest distractions are the magnificent views. Allow time to pull over and enjoy the scenery, and be aware that others may be distracted by the views too. Another hazard is wildlife such as bears and deer, which may dash onto the road with little notice. Fog sometimes envelops the roadway, especially at the higher elevations; please slow down in foggy conditions. When it is snowy or icy, avoid driving if possible, and remember that tire chains or cables are required.

Always let someone know when you go for a hike. Dress in layers, and carry rain gear and plenty of water, as weather conditions can change rapidly. Be aware of fast-moving streams and waterfalls. Falling trees and branches can present hazards. Rockfalls can present a significant hazard in the park, especially in Yosemite Valley. Thin air at elevations higher than

In winter, Yosemite offers quiet solitude as well as opportunities to enjoy the season.

8,000 feet increases the chance of mountain sickness; symptoms include headaches, nausea, and dizziness. Typically, your body adjusts to high altitudes after about two or three days, but if you experience symptoms of mountain sickness, move to a lower elevation (see "Elevations of Common Park Destinations"). Prevent dehydration and sunburn, respectively, by drinking plenty of water and applying sunscreen. Do not drink untreated water from springs or streams; the seemingly clean water may harbor parasites including *Giardia lamblia*, which causes severe diarrhea.

Never feed wildlife. Not only is it illegal but it also endangers the welfare of the animal. Stay a safe distance from all wildlife. There are rattlesnakes and scorpions in some part of the park; be careful where you place your hands and feet, especially when climbing on rocks or in shrubby areas.

Although there are no grizzly bears here, black bears do reside in the park. Most will avoid you if they hear you coming. Remain at least fifty yards from bears. If you encounter a bear, make your presence known by talking quietly and slowly back away. If the bear approaches you make noise by yelling and clapping your hands. Avoid hiking alone, and never let small children run ahead of you on trails. Keep them beside you and pick them up if you see a bear on or near the trail.

Yosemite black bears are smart, curious, and very determined. They know that humans bring food with them, and some will do anything to get to it—even to the point of breaking into your car. Food items include anything with a scent, including toiletries, sunscreen, lip balm, trash, canned food, drinks, and even empty ice chests. Proper food storage is required in Yosemite, and bear-proof food lockers are available at campgrounds and most trailhead parking areas. Bear-resistant food containers must be used when backpacking.

Ticks and mosquitoes are most active at dawn and dusk; use insect repellent and tuck your pants into your socks to prevent bites that may result in Lyme disease or West Nile virus. If you find a tick attached to you, remove it by pulling steadily with a tissue covering your fingers, and then clean the bite. See a health care provider if you develop a rash or become ill. Deer mice may carry hantavirus, which can cause Hantavirus Pulmonary Syndrome (HPS). If you see evidence of rodent activity in your room or other facility, contact park staff immediately.

Poison oak may be encountered along trails; learn to recognize this three-leaved plant. If you come in contact with poison oak, wash the affected area with cool water.

Please report emergencies such as accidents, uncontrolled fires, or other safety hazards by calling (209) 379-1992 or 911.

Note: Any references to ethnobotanical or edible uses of plants or fungi in this book are for academic purposes only; many plants and fungi are poisonous or otherwise harmful.

Conservation Note

Please leave wildflowers and other plants where they grow. When hiking, stay on established trails and watch where you put your feet to avoid damaging plants. Especially in cliff areas, avoid trampling plants and lichens, as some of them may only be able to exist in these special conditions. It is illegal to pick, dig, or damage any plant. Please report any suspicious activity, such as plant poaching, to a park ranger. Remember that all natural resources are protected in the park, including the rocks, minerals, and pinecones. Please leave them for others to observe and enjoy.

How to Use This Book

Common and Scientific Name

In an effort to create consistent communication worldwide, each organism has been given a Latin name—designated as genus and species—that is unique to that organism. Common names of families are given, with the scientific family name in parentheses. In many cases an organism may have many common names, often varying in locality. In addition, genetic research is rapidly discovering new inherent relationships and associations, and the taxonomic status of many organisms may change with the new information. In general, organisms are listed taxonomically according to conventional standards or alphabetically by order, Latin family name, and then genus.

Photo Tips

With jaw-dropping scenery at every turn, Yosemite's grandeur inspires the photographer in each of us. If you enter the park from the South Entrance, your first view into Yosemite Valley is from Tunnel View, which is undoubtedly one of the most photographed scenes in the United States. For those entering the park from the other entrances, before you head up to Tunnel View, stop

No matter how tempting, please remember never to feed wildlife.

at the Ansel Adams Gallery in Yosemite Village to see the inspiring work of Ansel Adams, whose photographic eye for beauty inspired the nation until his death in 1984.

For crystal-sharp scenics, a tripod is necessary, especially for low-light conditions in the early morning or evening. Sharp focus is the key to taking great nature photos. Overcast days offer nice soft lighting for wildflowers and animals. In deep shade, increase the ISO or use a flash. Bright sunny days create harsh shadows, and a flash is needed to add detail to the dark shaded areas of the flower or to add a speck of light to the eye.

Image stabilization capability will help reduce blur from camera motion. With more advanced camera systems, shooting close-ups at f16 with a flash will stop motion and provide more depth of field. When taking wildflower photos, be careful not to trample other plants.

Use a telephoto lens to zoom in on wildlife, and be sure to keep the animal's eyes in focus. Never approach wildlife too closely just to get a picture. If your behavior changes the behavior of the animal, you are too close.

Proper storage of food is required in Yosemite to help keep wildlife wild.

Suggested Nature Hikes and Wildlife Viewing Areas in or near Yosemite National Park

The following areas or trails are suggested for the general public and families who want to see wildlife, wildflowers, and other natural features of Yosemite National Park. Some of the recommended trails are wheelchair accessible or accessible with assistance. Of course the wild animals and plants of the park may not always be where expected, so it is a good idea to first stop at a visitor center and check with a park ranger about recent sightings. To find other hikes you might find attractive, consult a topographic map or hiking guides such as *Best Easy Day Hikes Yosemite National Park* and *Hiking Yosemite National Park* (FalconGuides). These and other interpretive publications are sold at park visitor centers. The park website has printable maps of certain popular areas in the park (www.nps.gov/yose/planyourvisit/hiking.htm).

Always maintain a safe distance from and never feed wildlife. Remember, you are more likely to see wild animals during the early morning and evening, when they are more active. Do not pick wildflowers or remove any natural objects from the park. Pets are not allowed on certain trails; check with a park ranger for pet regulations,

Cautious driving can prevent wildlife accidents.

Yosemite's iconic geologic formations provide stunning photographic opportunities.

or check the park website: www.nps.gov/yose/planyourvisit/pets.htm. The Yosemite Conservancy (yosemiteconservancy.org) offers Outdoor Adventures led by experienced naturalists—what better way to learn about the nature of Yosemite National Park?

Yosemite Valley. The number one destination of visitors to Yosemite National Park is Yosemite Valley. The hub of the park, Yosemite Valley is full of granite domes, plunging waterfalls, and abundant natural features. Rock climbers flock to the park for its many climbing challenges, including the world-famous El Capitan and Half Dome. In spring, when the waterfalls are at their best, Cooks Meadow is alive with butterflies, which gather nectar at the colorful wildflowers. Summer's sun warms the young fawns and cubs that explore the meadows and forests, and ground squirrels entertain visitors with their antics. Come fall, acorns drop off the oaks and mule deer browse heavily, fattening up before the cold sets in. Winter is the quiet time and one of the best times to visit the Valley to see birds that live here year-round, including the clown-like acorn woodpeckers.

Mariposa Grove. About 500 massive giant sequoia trees are the stars here. Hiking trails through the grove provide visitors with an up-close look at these giants, including the California Tunnel Tree and the Grizzly Giant. Many other plants and animals reside among the sequoias, including chickarees, pileated woodpeckers, and mule deer. Located near the South Entrance to Yosemite off CA 41 near Oakhurst, the 2-mile Mariposa Grove Road is open approximately April through November, but the small parking lot fills quickly. The best option is to take the free shuttle bus from Wawona (check the park website for availability). In summer there is also a narrated tram ride available that winds its way through the grove. In winter, when the road is closed, you can snowshoe or ski into the grove from the South Entrance.

Glacier Point. Touted as the best view in the Sierra Nevada, Glacier Point overlooks Yosemite Valley, which lies over 3,000 feet at its base. The road to Glacier Point climbs past flower-filled meadows and pine and fir forests. On the way to the top, watch for coyotes, which are commonly seen along the road. At the top, lichen-splashed red firs and Jeffrey pines dominate the forests where chipmunks and chickarees scamper about searching for food. Shrubs that line the trails include manzanita, chinquapin, and huckleberry oak. From your vantage point, watch for soaring birds, including the world's fastest flyer, the peregrine falcon. In winter the road is only plowed as far as Badger Pass ski area.

Wawona. Wawona (pronounced "wuh-WO-nah") is a lovely area in Yosemite near the South Entrance. Containing the only golf course in a national park, the Pioneer Yosemite History Center, and the historic Wawona Hotel, the area provides a view of the park that is not evident elsewhere. The nature of Wawona can best be explored by an easy 3.5-mile hike on the Meadow Loop Trail. The shaded trail circles Wawona Meadow and follows an old dirt road that is mostly flat. Along the way look for wildflowers including trillium, striped coral root orchids, snow plant, and pinedrops. Mule deer are commonly seen grazing in the meadow, especially at dawn or dusk, and California quail may quietly slip past you on the trail.

Hetch Hetchy. A hike across O'Shaughnessy Dam leads you to cool waterfalls and lush mountain meadows filled with wildflowers in spring. At this low elevation, summer's heat makes hiking a challenge, but spring and fall are beautiful, allowing visitors an avenue into the northwest portion of the park. As you hike along the trail, watch for colorful spring bloomers such as yerba santa, harlequin lupines, columbines, and monkeyflowers. Butterflies enjoy many of the blooms, and colorful dragonflies alight on grasses, while swallows dip endlessly over the water.

Crane Flat. Although most people know Crane Flat only as a place to gas up their cars or stop for a snack, the Crane Flat area is worth exploring. The lush meadows, sometimes called flats, are filled with wildflowers including pink shooting stars, white orchids, orange tiger lilies, yellow coneflowers, green corn lilies, tall yellow California cornflowers, and purple agastaches. The meadows are also a great place to watch for black bears, which like to eat the lush vegetation. Birding is great here too, so watch for brown creepers, Lincoln's sparrows, red-winged blackbirds, red-breasted nuthatches, and common ravens. About 4 miles past Crane Flat on Big Oak Flat Road is the trailhead to the Merced Grove of Giant Sequoias. One mile east of Crane Flat on the Tioga Road, you can take a hike to the Tuolumne Grove of Giant Sequoias.

Tioga Road. The drive along Tioga Road takes about 2 hours without stopping, but with its jaw-dropping scenery and unique subalpine habitat, you should plan plenty of extra time to enjoy the ride. About 15 miles from Crane Flat, you will see signs for the road to White Wolf. This area is famous for lush meadows of summer wildflowers. About 12 miles past the White Wolf turnoff is the road to the May Lake Trailhead, where you can see tiny fairy shrimp dancing about in the pond at the parking area. May Lake is the location for one of the park's High Sierra Camps, and the 1.2-mile trail climbs granite slopes into the camp at 9,330 feet elevation. The picturesque turnout about a mile from the May Lake Road is Olmstead Point, where you can take a short hike on a nature trail. Yellow-bellied marmots are common here. About 2 miles past Olmstead Point, Tenaya Lake is a great place to stop for a picnic while enjoying the scenery. Passing high-altitude meadows including Tuolumne and Dana Meadows at a breathtaking altitude of 9,943 feet, the road finally climbs through Tioga Pass before descending into the eastern flank of the Sierra Nevada, where you can watch for small birds called gray-crowned rosy finches along high-altitude road and snowfield edges. (*Note:* The Tioga Road is closed in winter.)

Tuolumne Meadows. Pronounced "too-AH-lum-ee," this subalpine meadow is one of Yosemite National Park's unobtrusive gems. Backpackers often begin their wilderness treks here on the many trails that lead into the Sierra Nevada, including the John Muir and the Pacific Crest Trails. Here you can see Pothole and Lembert Domes, which show such obvious signs of glaciation as scouring, chatter marks, potholes, and erratics (boulders left behind by retreating glaciers). The displays at the Tuolumne Meadows Visitor Center are a great way to learn about the geology and nature of the area. Kids of all ages will enjoy the activities of the Junior Ranger program. The Tuolumne River that winds through the meadow is home to trout that thrive in the cold mountain water. Butterflies such as fritillaries and Sierra Nevada blues take advantage of the nectar offered by the short-season flowers here, including bistorts, goldenrods, and asters. The consistent pips and squeaks of Belding ground squirrels in the meadow help warn their relatives of threats, such as the hawks that hunt small mammals.

Natural Areas outside Yosemite National Park

Mono Lake. Located on US 395 near the town of Lee Vining and about 13 miles east of Yosemite National Park, Mono Lake is one of the oldest lakes in the Western Hemisphere. More than twice as salty as the ocean, the lake's extreme conditions have created hauntingly beautiful geologic formations called tufas (pronounced "TOO-fahs"). Designated a globally significant Important Bird Area by the American Bird Conservancy and the Audubon Society, the Mono Lake area attracts thousands of birds that feast on swarms of alkali flies and brine shrimp in the lake. Birders come here from around the world to view the avian show. The Mono

Basin National Forest Scenic Area Visitor Center has interactive displays and nature trails. Make sure to check out the clickable online Eastern Sierra Birding Trail Map at easternsierrabirding trail.org/map.htm. For more information contact the Mono Lake Committee (760-647-6377; monolake.org) or Lee Vining Chamber of Commerce (760-647-6629; leevining.com).

Devils Postpile National Monument. About a 3 hour drive from Yosemite Valley via Tioga Road (closed in winter) and about 1 hour south of Lee Vining on the east side of the park, Devils Postpile National Monument (nps.gov/depo/index.htm) is a must for geology lovers. The park protects one of the finest examples of columnar basalt, some of the columns towering 60 feet high. From Lee Vining take US 395 to CA 203 into Mammoth Lakes.

Sequoia & Kings Canyon National Parks. About 3.5 hours south of Yosemite National Park, Sequoia National Park has abundant wildlife and botanical gems of giant sequoia groves, including a fallen sequoia that you can drive through in your car. At the Giant Forest Sequoia Grove and Grant Grove, you can get an up-close view of some of the biggest trees on Earth, including the world's largest, the General Sherman Tree. Don't miss a fascinating look beneath the park with a guided tour into the marble depths of Crystal Cave. Drive into Mineral King, where you can hike into the alpine zone, which also includes Mount Whitney—at 14,494 feet, the highest mountain in the contiguous United States. Adjoining Sequoia National Park is Kings Canyon National Park. Drive down into this spectacular glacially carved U-shaped canyon, with walls 3,500 feet above the canyon floor (www.nps.gov/seki/index.htm).

Renowned conservationist John Muir worked to promote Yosemite to national park status.

Ecosystems

Although many people would describe California with visions of the warm, sunny beaches of California's coastline, the state has

Beauty abounds in hidden places for those who take time to notice.

surprisingly varied ecosystems. Much of this variation is due to the presence of a large mountain chain called the Sierra Nevada. Running north to south, these rugged mountains were formed from collisions of deep underground plates that still rumble and groan as they press together, causing the numerous earthquakes associated with the state.

Yosemite's last glaciers melted away about 20,000 years ago, leaving the granite-carved valleys and domes we know today. The tallest mountains soar more than 10,500 feet into the sky, where only the hardiest plants and animals can survive the harsh alpine conditions. But in just a 2-hour drive, you can be in the foothill zone with near desertlike conditions. The subalpine zone and the upper and lower montane zones add an amazing diversity of habitats where the shrubs, trees, wildflowers, and animals each survive in their own particular niches.

Geology

Granite forms when molten rock, called magma, cools underground and eventually solidifies into solid rock. Most of the mountains you see all around you are composed of granite that has been sculpted by the actions of mighty glaciers. Geologists tell us that Half Dome was once a larger dome that was partially

Waterfalls (Bridalveil Fall)

sculpted away due to the work of glaciers combined with the properties of granite that cause it to break away in layers.

Glaciers formed the U-shaped valleys characteristic of Yosemite Valley and Hetch Hetchy. Evidence of glaciers can be seen in glacial polish and C-shaped chatter marks, where the debris-laden glaciers slid past the bedrock. When glaciers melt, they leave behind large solitary boulders called erratics, as seen along Tioga Road and Olmstead Point. Hanging waterfalls such as Yosemite, Bridalveil, Sentinel, and Ribbon were formed by powerful glaciers that scraped away the original rock wall. Talus slopes and large boulders from rockfalls are commonly seen in Yosemite Valley. Weathering, water, earthquakes, and other natural mechanisms can trigger rockfalls. Domes in Yosemite are formed by exfoliation of granite slabs and by glacial abrasion. Exfoliation of rocks like granite is a bit like peeling the layers off an onion. Sentinel Dome in Yosemite Valley was formed by exfoliation, but Lembert Dome in Tuolumne Meadows was formed primarily by glaciation.

U-shaped valley (Yosemite Valley)

COYOTE
Canis latrans
Dog family (Canidae)
Quick ID: medium-size, doglike appearance; gray to reddish coat; pointed erect ears; long slender snout; black-tipped tail usually carried straight down
Length: 2.5–3.3' Weight: 15–44 lb

About the size of a medium-size dog, coyotes are commonly mistaken for wolves, which are not found in Yosemite. One of the most adaptable of all animals, the coyote has expanded its range from western states into the East, where is it now a common resident. In the wild, coyotes feed mainly on small mammals including rodents and rabbits but will also eat a wide variety of plants and fruits. Opportunistic and intelligent, they soon discover that human food and garbage may be easily obtained and will take advantage of unsecured picnic leftovers. Never feed any wild animal in the park, and make sure to store food and garbage in scavenger-proof containers.

GRAY FOX
Urocyon cinereoargenteus
Dog family (Canidae)
Quick ID: salt-and-pepper grizzled-gray back; rusty side, neck, legs, and feet; dark streak on back and tail; black-tipped tail
Length: 21–29" Weight: 7–13 lb

About the size of a miniature poodle, the gray fox is the only member of the dog family that can climb trees. Slightly smaller than the red fox, the gray fox also has a fluffy 11- to 16-inch-long black-tipped tail rather than the white-tipped tail of the red fox. Most active at dusk and dawn, they are sometimes seen foraging for insects and small mammals. Small numbers of a unique subspecies of red fox are also found in the park. The Sierra Nevada red fox (*Vulpes vulpes necator*) is threatened in the state of California, and park biologists are studying the high-altitude habitats where this fox may be found.

AMERICAN BEAVER
Castor canadensis
Beaver family (Castoridae)
Quick ID: dark brown; broad flat tail
Length: 3–3.9' Weight: 35–50 lb

Widely recognized by its large flat paddle-shaped tail, the American beaver is the natural engineer of the water world. Cutting trees with its large chisel-like teeth, the beaver constructs dams and lodges in streams, creating its own private fishing area and home. Adept at conserving oxygen, these aquatic specialists can remain submerged for 15 minutes. Beavers have a unique digestive system that allows them to digest bark and cambium, the inner layer of wood under the bark. They have a symbiotic relationship with microorganisms in their intestines that digest cellulose. Watch for beavers along streams and near Mirror Lake in Yosemite Valley.

MULE DEER
Odocoileus hemionus
Deer family (Cervidae)
Quick ID: grayish-brown to red-brown; white rump patch; black-tipped tail; male—forked antlers in fall
Length: 4.1–5.5' Weight: 66–200 lb

Seemingly too small for its ears, the mule deer gained its name from the resemblance of its oversize ears to those of a mule. Commonly seen in Yosemite Valley, Wawona, and Tuolumne Meadows, these deer have excellent hearing and good eyesight. They migrate to lower elevations in winter. Mule deer browse on leaves and tender twigs from shrubs and are especially fond of the nutritious acorns that grow on black oak trees. Elk are not found in Yosemite, and the only other animal in the park that is similar to the mule deer is the endangered Sierra Nevada bighorn sheep (*Ovis canadensis sierra*), which has curved horns and can only be found in remote areas of the park.

DEER MOUSE
Peromyscus maniculatus
Mice, rat, and vole family (Cricetidae)
Quick ID: grayish- to reddish-brown with white underparts; white feet; long bicolored tail; large beady eyes; large round ears
Length: body 2.8–4"; tail 2–5" Weight: .66–1.25 oz

A deer mouse has a long bicolored tail with a very clear delineation between the brown upper part and the white lower part. Deer mice can produce from two to four litters per year, typically with three to five young. The young grow rapidly and are capable of breeding about forty-nine days later. An important foundation in the ecological food chain, these and other rodents are an important source of protein for a wide variety of predators, including hawks, owls, raccoons, and snakes. Found throughout the United States, some deer mice carry Sin Nombre virus, a strain of hantavirus that causes severe respiratory symptoms. Keep food in sealed containers, and report indoor rodent activity to park staff.

BOBCAT
Lynx rufus
Cat family (Felidae)
Quick ID: tawny to gray with black spots and bars; ear tufts; short tail with black tip on top and white underneath
Length: 2.2–3.75' Weight: 11–33 lb

Although rarely seen, bobcats are a fairly common inhabitant of Yosemite National Park. Their dark markings, short bobbed tail, and relatively small size help differentiate this member of the cat family from the much larger mountain lion, which has a very long tail. Active mainly at dawn and dusk, bobcats' keen senses of sight and smell help them locate prey such as rodents, squirrels, and other small mammals. While resting and sleeping, they seek shelter in hollow trees, rock piles, and brush piles. Solitary animals, bobcats mark their territory by scent marking and scratching on a tree or log. Look for bobcats in forested areas of the park, including Yosemite Valley.

MOUNTAIN LION
Puma concolor
Cat family (Felidae)
Quick ID: uniform tawny brown with no spots (except as young); whitish underparts; very long black-tipped tail
Length: 6–8'   Weight: 88–220 lb

Although mountain lions are one of the largest predators in Yosemite National Park, they are also secretive and rarely seen. The more common bobcat is much smaller and has a "bobbed" tail that pales in comparison to the elegant 2-foot-long tail of the mountain lion. These large cats have a variety of common names, including panther, cougar, puma, and catamount. Common prey includes mule deer, rabbits, squirrels, and other small mammals. Mountain lions normally avoid human contact, but as people encroach on their habitat, encounters are inevitable. Do not let children run ahead of you on trails. If attacked, pick up children and fight back. Do not hike, bike, or jog alone, especially at dawn, dusk, or nighttime.

MOUNTAIN POCKET GOPHER
Thomomys monticola
Pocket gopher family (Geomyidae)
Quick ID: brown, chunky, mole-like; large forefeet with long claws; small eyes; small ears; short, nearly hairless tail
Length: 7.5–8.6" Weight: 1.8–3.7 oz

Resembling a chunky mole, pocket gophers spend most of their days in underground tunnels. Unlike the tiny teeth and eyes of moles, the teeth of pocket gophers are long and their eyes small but obvious. Infrequently seen aboveground, they subsist on roots, leaves, and other vegetable matter, which they cut off with their large front teeth and carry to underground storage areas in their fur-lined cheek pouches, or "pockets." Their front claws are used to excavate extensive tunnels through the soil. Evidence of their winter foraging under the snow is revealed in spring meadows by long rounded mounds of earth called gopher cores or eskers. A valued ecosystem component, pocket gopher tunnels capture water runoff, which helps maintain lush mountain meadows.

STRIPED SKUNK
Mephitis mephitis
Skunk family (Mephitidae)
Quick ID: black with 2 broad white stripes along back; large bushy tail with variable black and white
Length: 22–31.5" Weight: 6–14 lb

One of the most recognized creatures in the animal world, skunks are renowned for their defense mechanism. When threatened, they spew a stream of oily, foul-smelling liquid a distance of up to 10 feet, causing burning of the eyes and nose and nausea for the unfortunate victim. Victims of a blast of skunk spray can find relief by washing with a mixture of 3 percent hydrogen peroxide, a quarter cup of baking soda, and some liquid dishwashing soap, but it may change hair color. The home remedy of bathing in tomato juice only masks the scent. The smaller spotted skunk (*Spilogale putorius*) will stand on its front feet before spraying.

AMERICAN MARTEN
Martes americana
Weasel and otter family (Mustelidae)
Quick ID: weasel-like with pointed face and rounded ears; brownish; head and belly paler;
buffy-orange chest or throat; long bushy tail
Length: 19.5–26.5" Weight: 0.6–2.7 lb

Commonly called the pine marten, the American marten is a member of
the weasel family. About the size of a small house cat, this agile mammal is
a treat to see as they move silently through the forest, often loping along
a fallen log or racing up trees. This small predator hunts insects, rodents,
and other small mammals and occasionally birds. While taking a rest on
a hike, be aware of your surroundings; small birds will often sound alarm
notes when a marten is close by. You can look for these mostly nocturnal
forest inhabitants in campgrounds and in areas such as White Wolf.

LONG-TAILED WEASEL
Mustela frenata
Weasel and otter family (Mustelidae)
Quick ID: brown back and sides with yellowish belly; feet brownish; black-tipped tail; turns white in winter
Length: 11–16.5" Weight: 0.2–1 lb

The long sinuous brown body, long neck, and rounded ears atop a triangular head are characteristics to help identify a weasel. Sometimes confused with the ermine, or short-tailed weasel (*M. erminea*), the long-tailed weasel is aptly named—its 3- to 6-inch-long black-tipped tail is often a third as long as the body. In winter, both species molt in white hairs that blend well with the snow and help camouflage them from both predators and prey. Long-tailed weasels prey on small mammals such as mice, voles, pocket gophers, and ground squirrels, helping to keep those populations in check. Both larger, the Pacific fisher (*Martes pennant*) and American badger (*Taxidea taxus*) are also found in the park.

AMERICAN PIKA
Ochotona princeps
Pika family (Ochotonidae)
Quick ID: grayish-brown; small rounded ears; short legs
Length: 6.5–8.5" Weight: 4–6.5 oz

The American pika (pronounced "PI-kah," or sometimes "PEE-kah") is a small rabbit relative resembling a guinea pig that lives in the high altitudes of Yosemite. A high-country specialist, the pika is found only where temperatures are cool enough to balance its high metabolism and body temperature. Sensitive to climate change, in summer pikas must move higher in altitude to stay cool enough for survival. Hikers in the high country will probably hear the high-pitched single beep call before they see this tiny rock climber that lives in colonies amid boulder fields. During summer days they busily gather vegetation to dry and then store in hay piles for the long winter, as they do not hibernate.

RACCOON
Procyon lotor
Raccoon family (Procyonidae)
Quick ID: grizzled brownish-gray; stocky body; pointed snout; black facial mask; 5–7 black rings on bushy 8–12" tail
Length: 18–28" Weight: 4–23 lb

The distinguishing black mask across the eyes and a bushy tail with black rings are characteristic marks of a raccoon. The black mask helps camouflage them during their nightly forages for wild foods, which include fruits, nuts, insects, rodents, and fish. Raccoons may be seen in Yosemite Valley and in the lower elevations of the park. A relative of the raccoon and sporting a similar striped tail, the ringtail (*Bassariscus astutus*) is much smaller, with a long slender body and long tail. Shy and elusive, the ringtail is very agile and catlike in behavior, so much so that it is sometimes called a ringtail cat.

YELLOW-BELLIED MARMOT
Marmota flaviventris
Squirrel family (Sciuridae)
Quick ID: grizzled brownish-yellow on back, yellowish belly; short bushy tail; whitish band across nose
Length: 1.5–2.2' Weight: 3.3–8.8 lb

Along Tioga Road, a stop at Olmstead Point affords visitors a phenomenal view of the high country and of the "back" of Half Dome. Olmstead Point is also a great place to watch for yellow-bellied marmots that pop up from the rocky slope below the parking area. You may hear their high-pitched chucks, whistles, and trills before you see them. Visitors from the East may confuse the yellow-bellied marmot with its relative, the groundhog. Marmots eat a wide variety of vegetation, and by fall they've accumulated enough fat reserves to keep them alive during their long winter hibernation. Look for these roly-poly high-altitude denizens in rocky areas adjacent to open areas such as Tuolumne Meadows and along May Lake Trail.

CALIFORNIA GROUND SQUIRREL
Otospermophilus beecheyi
Squirrel family (Sciuridae)
Quick ID: mottled gray, brown, and white fur; bushy tail; underside grayish-white; white eye ring
Length: body 9–11"; tail 5–9" Weight: 0.62–1.6 lb

Entertaining summer visitors, three species of ground squirrels can be found in Yosemite, including the California ground squirrel, which is commonly seen in Yosemite Valley and most areas of the park. They spend much of the year in underground burrows, but when spring arrives they begin busily feeding on seeds, acorns, fruits, roots, fungi, and insects. Constantly vigilant, they survey their territories by sitting straight up and squeaking alarms and call notes, much like prairie dogs, for which they are sometimes mistaken. When gathering food, they stuff their cheek pouches full to carry it back to their burrow. The larger western gray squirrel has a white belly and very bushy tail.

WESTERN GRAY SQUIRREL
Sciurus griseus
Squirrel family (Sciuridae)
Quick ID: salt-and-pepper gray above with white underparts; tail gray, edged with white
Length: body 9–12"; tail 10–12" Weight: 1.2–1.75 lb

Although not as commonly noticed as the lively California ground squirrels or noisy chickarees of the woodlands, the shy western gray squirrel is arguably the most attractive of all the squirrels in Yosemite. With its distinguished silvery gray coat atop a white belly and sporting a luxuriant long bushy tail edged with white, this squirrel is king of the fashion parade. These squirrels eat a variety of foods, including pine seeds, acorns, berries, fungi, and insects. Active year-round, they bury acorns in the fall to store for the long winter. When eating pinecone seeds, they often leave behind piles of cone scales and shreds of cones. Look for these beautiful squirrels in Yosemite Valley and areas such as Hodgdon Meadow.

BELDING'S GROUND SQUIRREL
Spermophilus beldingi
Squirrel family (Sciuridae)
Quick ID: grayish-brown tinged with yellow on sides; rusty-red coloration on back and tail, underside lighter; broken whitish ring around large black eye; small ears; small tail
Length: 9–12" Weight: 8–11 oz

Named for Lyman Belding (1829–1927) an early California natural-ist, Belding's ground squirrels live in colonies in open areas such as Tuolumne Meadows. These hardy ground squirrels survive the harsh high-altitude conditions by spending more than half the year hibernat-ing in underground burrows. Foraging on summer grasses and seeds, they are on constant guard, sitting upright like prairie dogs as they watch for predators such as hawks and weasels. This upright position earned them the nickname "picket pin" from their resemblance to a ground stake used to tether horses. These and other squirrels may be seen "kissing," but they are actually smelling secretions from a gland near the mouth to examine relatedness. Their loud alarm calls also vary slightly within family groups.

GOLDEN-MANTLED GROUND SQUIRREL
Spermophilus lateralis
Squirrel family (Sciuridae)
Quick ID: golden-reddish with whitish belly; no stripes on head; white ring around eye
Length: 9.5–11.5" Weight: 6–12 oz

Often misidentified as a large chipmunk, the golden-mantled ground squirrel can be differentiated from chipmunks by the fact that is does not have stripes on its head, as do all the chipmunks found in Yosemite. Golden-mantled ground squirrels also have a distinctive white ring around the eye and a russet-gold "mantle" on their neck and shoulders. Found throughout the park, these squirrels are fairly omnivorous, eating a wide variety of foods including fungi, plants, fruits, seeds, insects, eggs, small mammals, and carrion. Like the other ground squirrels in the park, in fall they hibernate in underground burrows.

DOUGLAS'S SQUIRREL
Tamiasciurus douglasii
Squirrel family (Sciuridae)
Quick ID: reddish- to grayish-brown; underparts rusty to buffy-gray; lateral black stripe on side in summer; white ring around eye; slight hair tufts on ears
Length: 12.9–14.9" Weight: 7–10.5 oz

Tiny sentinels of the forests, Douglas's squirrels, or, as they are commonly called, chickarees, loudly announce intruders with trills, chirps, barks, and clicks that ring through the treetops. Often mistaken as calling birds or large chipmunks, the chatters of these fiery sprites can be heard throughout Yosemite in coniferous forests, where they forage for berries, mushrooms, and the seeds of conifers. Their foraging habits play a vital role in forest ecology by spreading seeds and fungal spores for regrowth. Douglas's squirrel was named to honor David Douglas (1799–1834), a Scottish naturalist who explored the plants and animals of California in the early 1800s. Look for chickarees in sequoia groves and other forested areas of the park.

LODGEPOLE CHIPMUNK
Tamias speciosus
Squirrel family (Sciuridae)
Quick ID: sides of body reddish-brown; black head stripes with outer stripes white; light patch behind ear
Length: 7.7–8.5" Weight: 1.1–2.2 oz

Thirteen species of chipmunks are found in California, and Yosemite National Park is home to six of these. All chipmunks have stripes on their head and face, which helps tell them apart from their look-alike cousins, chickarees (*Tamiasciurus douglasii*) and golden-mantled ground squirrels (*Spermophilus lateralis*). Different species of chipmunks are characterized by slight variances in size, color, and markings; the elevation at which a particular chipmunk is found also can help with identification. Merriam's chipmunk (*T. merriami*) is found at lowest elevations, followed by long-eared (*T. quadrimaculatus*), yellow-pine (*T. amoenus*), and Allen's (*T. senex*). Lodgepole chipmunks are commonly seen at Glacier Point. Global warming has forced the alpine chipmunk (*T. alpinus*), endemic to California, to climb over 1,600 feet higher in elevation to survive.

BLACK BEAR
Ursus americanus
Bear family (Ursidae)
Quick ID: large, usually black to brownish; light brown snout; round ears; flat-footed walk
Length: 4–6.5' Weight: 86–690 lb

The excitement of seeing Yosemite's largest predator in the wild is a highlight for many visitors to the park. Even though the California state flag proudly displays the grizzly bear, the black bear is the only species of bear found in the state. Grizzlies have not existed here since the early 1920s, when the last one was shot outside the park. Black bears are primarily vegetarians and eat a wide variety of plants, berries, and nuts but quickly learn that human food and garbage make an easy meal. All visitors to the park are required to safely store their food, use bear-proof garbage containers, and never attempt to feed bears. Black bears are often seen in Yosemite Valley meadows.

BIG BROWN BAT
Eptesicus fuscus
Evening and Vesper bat family (Vespertilionidae)
Quick ID: large, 4–5" body length, 11–13" wingspan; glossy brown
Length: 4.1–4.7" Weight: 0.5–0.8 oz

In spite of a bad rap, these small flying mammals are an incredibly important part of the ecosystem. Of the seventeen bat species in Yosemite, the big brown bat is one of the most common. With astonishing voraciousness, big brown bats are known to eat as many as twenty insects per minute. Every night, bats find their insect prey by using a sonar-like method called echolocation, in which they emit a high-frequency sound wave that bounces back to them when it hits another object. When observing bats darting about the lights in Curry Village, admire their amazing ability to veer, dive, and rocket after moths, mosquitoes, and other flying insects that may otherwise end up in your tent.

GOLDEN EAGLE
Aquila chrysaetos
Diurnal raptor family (Accipitridae)
Quick ID: very large dark brown raptor; golden head; long wings
Length: 30" Weight: 10 lb Wingspan: 79"

As the largest aerial predator in the park, the golden eagle plays an important role in controlling populations of the small mammals that are its main prey. The tall granite cliffs in Yosemite are an important nesting site for these eagles. Golden eagles take three years to reach adult plumage; during this phase they are sometimes mistaken for young bald eagles (*Haliaeetus leucocephalus*). Juvenile golden eagles often have a white patch near the end of their wings as well as a white band on the tail. Majestically soaring over valleys, they hold their wings in a slight V, not unlike the smaller turkey vulture (*Cathartes aura*), which has a broad silvery sheen to the flight feathers.

RED-TAILED HAWK
Buteo jamaicensis
Diurnal raptor family (Accipitridae)
Quick ID: large, dark mottled-brown hawk; broad, rounded wings; reddish tail; streaked bellyband
Length: 19" Weight: 2.4 lb Wingspan: 49"

One of the most common hawks in North America, the upper red tail feathers can sometimes be seen when the red-tailed hawk banks gracefully on broad rounded wings. Juveniles don't acquire the red tail feathers until they are older and instead have brown and white tail bands. "Red-tails" are larger and heavier than red-shouldered hawks (*B. lineatus*), which have red barring covering their belly and distinctly barred tails. The much smaller sharp-shinned hawks (*Accipiter striatus*) are long tailed and have brown to blue-gray backs with horizontal reddish breast bars. A powerful raptor, the northern goshawk (*A. gentilis*) may be recognized by its large size, long tail, blue-gray back, gray belly, dark cap, and stripe through the eye.

RED-SHOULDERED HAWK
Buteo lineatus
Diurnal raptor family (Accipitridae)
Quick ID: dark wings with white checkered pattern; rusty-red shoulders; translucent buffy crescent across wingtips; rusty-red barring across white underparts
Length: 17" Weight: 1.4 lb Wingspan: 40"

Red-shouldered hawks are often seen perched in a tall tree at the edges of meadows or open spaces intently surveying the ground for small mammals, amphibians, or reptiles. These hawks can sometimes be seen soaring over Yosemite Valley meadows and can be quite vocal, calling with repeated whistled kee-aah notes. Juvenile red-shouldered hawks are brown overall, with heavy dark markings underneath and a broadly striped tail. Cooper's hawks (*Accipiter cooperii*) have much longer tails and shorter wings than red-shouldered hawks. Red-tailed hawks (*B. jamaicensis*) are larger, with a red tail and dark bellyband.

BELTED KINGFISHER
Megaceryle alcyon
Kingfisher family (Alcedinidae)
Quick ID: steel-blue back and face; shaggy crest on head; long pointed bill; white under-neath; short legs and tail; male—one dark chest band; female—upper breast band blue, lower breast band and sides rusty
Length: 13" Weight: 5 oz Wingspan: 20"

A harsh squirrel-like rattle call that can be clearly heard over rushing streams may be the first indication that a belted kingfisher is nearby. Experts at catching fish, kingfishers often perch on a shrub or tree limb near water, watching for an unsuspecting fish to swim by. Their attack is rapid and direct as they plunge-dive headfirst into the water to spear the fish on their dagger-like bills, which have backward serrations to help keep the fish from sliding off. Year-round residents of Yosemite, these adaptable birds are sometimes seen near open waters during the park's annual Christmas Bird Count.

COMMON MERGANSER
Mergus merganser
Duck, geese, swan family (Anatidae)
Quick ID: tapered orange-red bill; sloping forehead; male—greenish-black head, black back, white body; female—chestnut head and throat, white chin patch, gray breast
Length: 25" Weight: 3.4 lb Wingspan: 34"

Visitors seeking a peaceful moment in Yosemite Valley often find themselves at Swinging Bridge or Sentinel Bridge, where they may see ducks such as common mergansers and mallards floating quietly down the Merced River. Common mergansers have a distinctive pointed reddish-orange bill, and a large white wing patch is evident in flight. Male mallards also have a green head, but mallards have a flatter yellowish bill and dark chest. Female mallards are mottled brown, while merganser females have a brown head with grayish body. Other waterfowl sharing the waters of Yosemite include green-winged teal (*Anas crecca*), harlequin ducks (*Histrionicus histrionicus*), buffleheads (*Bucephala albeola*), and Canada geese (*Branta canadensis*).

WHITE-THROATED SWIFT
Aeronautes saxatalis
Swift family (Apodidae)
Quick ID: cylindrical body; long narrow pointed swept-back wings; black back, wings, and tail; white throat, belly, and sides; tail slightly forked; tiny feet
Length: 6.5" Weight: 1.1 oz Wingspan: 15"

In summer, white-throated swifts slice through the clear Yosemite skies over valleys and canyons on glider-like wings perfectly proportioned for aerial acrobatics. Swifts have the ability to flap their wings independently, surpassing the aerial agility of other birds. The flying talents of this small bird prompted its scientific genus name, *Aeronautes*, which is Greek for "sailor through the air." The species name, *saxatalis*, is derived from the Latin for "rock-inhabiting," in reference to its nesting sites on rocky cliffs. Black swifts (*Cypseloides niger*) and Vaux's swifts (*Chaetura vauxi*) can also be seen in the park, as well as species of the similar swallow, including violet-green (*Tachycineta thalassina*), cliff (*Petrochelidon pyrrhonota*), and barn (*Hirundo rustica*) swallows.

BLACK-HEADED GROSBEAK
Pheucticus melanocephalus
Cardinal family (Cardinalidae)
Quick ID: chunky; thick grayish bill; male—black head and tail, black wings with white patches, dull orange underparts and neckband; female—brown with heavy white streaks
Length: 8.25"   Weight: 1.6 oz   Wingspan: 12.5"

Foraging in the tall trees surrounding Ahwahnee Meadow, with their black and orange Halloween colors, black-headed grosbeaks light up the trees as the birds flit about picking insects from the green foliage. In the world of birds bill size and shape tells a lot about the eating habits of each species. For grosbeaks, their extremely stout bills are perfect for crushing open seeds and for chomping down on fruits and insects. Grosbeak is from the French word *grosbec*, which means "thick-billed." Females and young males lack the contrasting coloration of adult males and sport a subdued brown-and-white-stripe coloration. Male Bullock's orioles (*Icterus bullocki*) are also orange and black but have a decidedly pointed bill and orange on the face.

WESTERN TANAGER
Piranga ludoviciana
Cardinal family (Cardinalidae)
Quick ID: Male—reddish-orange head; bright yellow neck, rump, and underparts; back and tail black; wings black with yellow and white markings; female—olive-green upper-parts with back and wings gray; yellowish rump; pale yellow belly
Length: 7.25" Weight: 0.98 oz Wingspan: 11.5"

So colorful is the male western tanager that the first sight of one is often the spark that ignites a lifelong love for birds. The bright reddish-orange head and bright yellow body contrast strikingly with the black wings and tail. The female is rather dull olive-green to gray, which helps camouflage her when sitting on the nest. Most members of the tanager family reside year-round in warmer climates, but the western tanager migrates north in spring to breed in the western states and Canada. In fall they return to spend the winter in central Mexico, Costa Rica, and Southern California. Look for western tanagers in forested areas of Yosemite Valley.

AMERICAN DIPPER
Cinclus mexicanus
Dipper family (Cinclidae)
Quick ID: stocky gray body; relatively long legs; short tail; short pointed wings
Length: 7.5" Weight: 2 oz Wingspan: 11"

The lively behavior of this chunky, little gray songbird has made it the favorite of many nature lovers, including John Muir and President Theodore Roosevelt. Also commonly known as water ouzel (pronounced "OO-zuhl"), the American dipper is always found near cold fast-moving water. Dippers have a unique method of searching for aquatic insects and other food by diving headfirst under the water and then walking or even swimming upstream underwater. Dippers remain near open water, even in winter; you can watch for dippers as they fly over fast-moving water or dip and bob up and down while perched on a rock. These fascinating birds build dome-shaped nests on riverbanks and sometimes under bridges in the park, such as Swinging and Sentinel Bridges.

BAND-TAILED PIGEON
Patagioenas fasciata
Dove and pigeon family (Columbidae)
Quick ID: pale gray above, purplish-gray below; gray underwings with dark wingtips; pale band at tip of tail; white crescent on upper neck; yellow feet and bill
Length: 14.5" Weight: 13 oz Wingspan: 26"

Bolting noisily overhead, a flock of band-tailed pigeons may draw your attention skyward as they ply the air in large, loose groups. These pigeons are common in oak woodlands at lower elevations in the park, where they feed on seeds, fruits, and acorns. They have a slimmer, more streamlined look than the introduced rock doves (*Columba livia*) so common in towns and cities. Found in the Southwest and the Pacific coastal states, the band-tailed pigeon was a source of food for American Indians and early European settlers to the area.

COMMON RAVEN
Corvus corax
Crow and jay family (Corvidae)
Quick ID: large, solid black body; long narrow wings; wedge-shaped tail; heavy bill
Length: 24" Weight: 2.6 lb Wingspan: 53"

The object of myth, legend, and poetry, the common raven has few rivals in its avian notoriety. Noted for their ability to solve complex cause-and-effect problems, ravens have been the object of many scientific studies of intelligence. Their keen observation talents and advanced intellectual capabilities have placed ravens in a category with other highly advanced predators. Opportunistic feeders, these omnivores prey on a variety of small mammals, including chipmunks and ground squirrels. They also feed on carrion, plant materials, and garbage. In Yosemite, ravens are much more common than the American crow (*C. brachyrhynchos*). Also entirely black, crows are much smaller than ravens and have a short rounded tail as opposed to the wedge-shaped tail of the raven.

STELLER'S JAY
Cyanocitta stelleri
Crow and jay family (Corvidae)
Quick ID: azure blue body, wings, and tail; head, breast, and back blackish; long crest on head
Length: 11.5" Weight: 3.7 oz Wingspan: 19"

With its pointed crest and azure blue feathers, the Steller's jay is one of the easiest birds for beginning birders to recognize. The blue jay (*C. cristata*) of the eastern states is the only other jay with a crest, but it has white facial markings rather than the black markings of the Steller's jay. Fearless and smart, the Steller's jay's keen eye for an easy meal has earned it the dubious nickname "camp robber," and visitors to Yosemite often have to carefully watch their picnic table to avoid losing their food to these uninvited guests. The western scrub jay (*Aphelocoma californica*) can be seen at lower elevations in the park, such as near El Portal; also blue, it lacks the crest of the Steller's jay.

CLARK'S NUTCRACKER
Nucifraga columbiana
Crow and jay family (Corvidae)
Quick ID: pale gray body; black wings with white patch; pointed black bill; black tail with white outer tail feathers
Length: 12" Weight: 4.6 oz Wingspan: 24"

Named to honor William Clark of the famed Lewis and Clark Expedition, Clark's nutcrackers have a unique mutualistic relationship with a tree that is found only at high altitudes in the park. The gnarled branches of whitebark pines produce cones that hold the seed tightly inside until they are pried open by the strong, sharp bill of the Clark's nutcracker. A special pouch under the bird's tongue allows it to hold many seeds. These birds have been known to store thousands of seeds in hundreds of caches for later use. Even though this bird has a superior memory for finding the cached seeds, some remain to germinate into new whitebark pine trees. Look for Clark's nutcrackers along Tioga Road.

DARK-EYED JUNCO
Junco hyemalis
Sparrow family (Emberizidae)
Quick ID: gray to brown to blackish above; white belly; variable pinkish sides
Length: 6.25" Weight: 0.67 oz Wingspan: 9.25"

Dark-eyed juncos are a variable species with at least six different populations across the country. In Yosemite you can see two of these subspecies, Oregon and slate-colored. The more common Oregon junco (subspecies group *oreganus*) has contrasting coloration, with males sporting a blackish hood that contrasts sharply with the brown back. The female Oregon junco is duller, with a grayish hood. Juveniles resemble streaky sparrows, but unlike most sparrows, juncos flash white outer tail feathers in flight. The less-common slate-colored junco (subspecies group *hyemalis*) is slate gray with a white belly and pink bill. Juncos are frequently seen hopping about trailsides and open areas feeding on insects or seeds.

CALIFORNIA TOWHEE
Melozone crissalis
Sparrow family (Emberizidae)
Quick ID: grayish-brown overall; reddish-brown undertail feathers
Length: 9" Weight: 1.5 oz Wingspan: 11.5"

The song of many towhees resembles their common name, but the song of the California towhee is a sharp chip ending in a trill. Dull brown overall, these members of the sparrow family are highly camouflaged, but you may hear them scraping in the dirt for insects in brushy areas under shrubs and thickets. Found in similar habitats, the spotted towhee (*Pipilo maculatus*) has a distinguishing black head as well as a black back with white spots. The extremely secretive California thrasher (*Toxostoma redivivum*) is a thrush that is similar in coloration to the California towhee, but this bird of dry lowlands is larger and has a distinctive long, down-curved bill.

CHIPPING SPARROW
Spizella passerina
Sparrow family (Emberizidae)
Quick ID: brown back with black streaks; rufous crown; white eyebrow, black eye stripe; grayish breast; grayish rump
Length: 5.5" Weight: 0.42 oz Wingspan: 8.5"

Sparrow identification is often a challenge, even for experienced birders. Chipping sparrows can be identified by their rufous crown and black stripe through the eye with a white "eyebrow." The bright rufous cap helps to identify this small sparrow, but birds that were hatched this year often have less distinctly marked striped rufous caps and are paler overall. These small sparrows are often seen running on the ground hopping up to feed on grass seeds. Song sparrows (*Melospiza melodia*) are larger, with brown stripes overall and a central breast spot. Rufous-crowned (*Aimophila ruficeps*), fox (*Passerella iliaca*), and Lincoln's (*M. lincolnii*) sparrows may also be found in Yosemite.

WHITE-CROWNED SPARROW
Zonotrichia leucophrys
Sparrow family (Emberizidae)
Quick ID: bold black and white stripes on cap; unstreaked grayish breast, brown-streaked back; pinkish to yellow bill; immature—rusty crown
Length: 7" Weight: 1 oz Wingspan: 9.5"

A common sparrow of North America, the white-crowned sparrow is easily recognized by the clean white and black stripes on its cap. As with many species of sparrows, the juveniles are paler overall with brown markings rather than distinct black and white stripes on the cap. Sparrows spend much of their day hunting for seeds and insects and tend to forage close to shrubby areas, where they can dash for protection when threatened. Song sparrows (*Melospiza melodia*) have a streaked breast; fox sparrows (*Passerella iliaca*) are reddish overall. Golden-crowned sparrows (*Z. atricapilla*) have a central golden stripe on their head. Chipping sparrows (*Spizella passerina*) are quite small and have a clear gray breast and rusty cap.

PEREGRINE FALCON
Falco peregrinus
Falcon family (Falconidae)
Quick ID: large and stocky; gray barring; black cap; black mustache; long pointed wings
Length: 16" Weight: 1.6 lb Wingspan: 41"

Once teetering on the brink of extinction, the peregrine falcon is again plying the blue skies over Yosemite. Due to effects of the pesticide DDT, peregrine falcon populations reached perilously low numbers in the 1960s, but thanks to conservation efforts they recovered and in 2009 were removed from the California threatened and endangered species list. About half the size of the peregrine, American kestrels (*F. sparverius*) have a reddish back and often bob their tail when perched. The prairie falcon (*F. mexicanus*) is brown with white behind the eye and has a spotted white belly. Look for peregrines soaring near undisturbed cliff faces in the park.

CASSIN'S FINCH
Haemorhous cassinii
Finch family (Fringillidae)

Quick ID: brown-streaked back, wings, and tail; slightly peaked head feathers; male—red crown, chest, and markings; female—crisp brown and white streaks on underparts, thin white eye ring

Length: 6.25" Weight: 0.91 oz Wingspan: 11.5"

Joined by two other look-alike finches, the Cassin's finch is a common bird of western states. They often gather in small flocks foraging for berries, seeds, and insects. The purple finch (*H. purpureus*) male is bright rosy pink overall; the female has coarse brown and white stripes. The house finch (*H. mexicanus*) male has paler red feathers than the Cassin's male and has faint, blurry streaks on the sides. The female house finch is dull grayish brown with blurry streaks underneath. The small pine siskin (*Spinus pinus*) has brown streaks, with a tinge of yellow on the wings and tail and a sharp pointed bill.

GRAY-CROWNED ROSY-FINCH
Leucosticte tephrocotis
Finch family (Fringillidae)
Quick ID: streaked brown; head mostly gray with dark forehead; rosy feather patches on wings and sides
Length: 6.25" Weight: 0.91 oz Wingspan: 13"

Rosy-finches are small songbirds that spend their lives in high altitudes of western North America. Of the three types of rosy-finches—black, brown-capped, and gray-crowned—the gray-crowned rosy-finches can be found in Yosemite. At home in alpine regions of the park, the gray-crowned rosy-finch is one of the most sought-after sightings for avid birders. Almost always seen in small to large flocks, rosy-finches forage for insects at the edges of snowfields. In winter they eat seeds from grasses, sedges, and dried flower heads. Look for these birds in the Tioga Pass area and along high-elevation trails.

RED-WINGED BLACKBIRD
Agelaius phoeniceus
Blackbird family (Icteridae)
Quick ID: sharp pointed bill; male—shiny black, yellow bordered red on shoulder; female—streaky brown overall, puffy-orange throat
Length: 8.75" Weight: 1.8 oz Wingspan: 13"

The red-winged blackbird is one of the most widespread and numerous of all North American birds. Males arrive in early spring, and their loud repeated ko-ka-reeee calls are used to proclaim their territories in marshes and wet meadows. Visitors often accurately describe these conspicuous vocalists as black birds with red shoulder patches. Males spend much of their day vigorously defending their harems of up to ten females. Resembling large brown-streaked sparrows, red-winged females look nothing like the males. Females build a cup-shaped nest, binding it to surrounding grasses or shrubs. Look for red-winged blackbirds in lush meadows, such as Cook's Meadow in Yosemite Valley.

BREWER'S BLACKBIRD
Euphagus cyanocephalus
Blackbird family (Icteridae)
Quick ID: pointed black bill; relatively long legs; male—dark glossy purplish black with yellow eye; female—light brown with dark eye
Length: 9" Weight: 2.2 oz Wingspan: 15.5"

Named for Thomas Mayo Brewer, an early 1800s ornithologist, Brewer's blackbird is one of the most commonly seen birds in Yosemite. Glistening purple and green in the sunlight, the glossy black coloration of the male is striking; that of the female is a subdued light brown, which helps camouflage them when nesting. The male has a conspicuous yellow eye in contrast to the dark eye of the female. They use their straight conical bills to crack small seeds and to eat insects. Brewer's blackbirds migrate to warmer areas in winter, but during spring through fall they are frequently seen throughout Yosemite in all but the highest elevations.

MOUNTAIN QUAIL
Oreortyx pictus
New World quail family (Odontophoridae)
Quick ID: brown to gray, heavy white bars on chestnut sides, rusty under short tail, chestnut throat lined with white; long straight black plume
Length: 11"   Weight: 8 oz   Wingspan: 16"

The striking plumage of the mountain quail is a treat to see if one is lucky enough to catch a glimpse. Shy and secretive, they are ever watchful and constantly aware of their surroundings. Their ability to "freeze" at any sign of danger helps them blend into the manzanita and other shrubs that offer them shelter and protection. Mountain quail often travel together in a small group called a covey and will scurry into dense vegetation if startled. Their long straight plume that sometimes hangs backward differs from the forward-curved plume of the California quail. Look for mountain quail in Yosemite Valley and in the Foresta area.

CALIFORNIA QUAIL
Callipepla californica
New World quail family (Odontophoridae)
Quick ID: tends to walk on the ground; chunky; grayish-brown, white streaks on sides; scaly underparts; forward-curved dark "topknot" on head
Length: 10" Weight: 6 oz Wingspan: 14"

The California, or valley, quail is the official state bird of California. Their distinctive forward-curved topknot and plump grayish-brown body helps to identify these birds. Also found in the park, the mountain quail has a straight plume. To help remember the difference between the two quail, you can remember the name California by their C-shaped plume. The distinctive plume looks like one feather but is actually composed of six overlapping feathers. Outside the park, the California quail is an important game bird hunted for food. Both species were an important food source for the Miwok in Yosemite. Look for California quail in oak woodlands such as those in the Wawona area.

MOUNTAIN CHICKADEE
Poecile gambeli
Chickadee and titmouse family (Paridae)
Quick ID: gray back; buffy-white underparts; gray wings; black cap; white cheeks; black chin; white eyebrow; black line through eye
Length: 5.25" Weight: 0.39 oz Wingspan: 8.5"

You may hear the lively chick-a-dee-dee and fee-bee calls of the mountain chickadee before you notice this small, scrappy bird as it clings acrobatically to twigs or conifer cones foraging for insects. Chickadees eat large numbers of insects, including bark beetles and needle miners that infect trees. In autumn they busily cache conifer seeds for the winter ahead. The chestnut-backed chickadee (*P. rufescens*) can also be found at low elevations in Yosemite but in far lower numbers. Chestnut-backed chickadees lack the white eyebrow of the mountain chickadee and have chestnut sides and back. Mountain chickadees sometimes travel with other small birds, including tiny golden-crowned kinglets (*Regulus satrapa*), brown creepers (*Certhia americana*), and oak titmice (*Baeolophus inornatus*).

YELLOW-RUMPED WARBLER
Setophaga coronata
Wood warbler family (Parulidae)
Quick ID: large warbler; white spots in tail; male—gray back with black markings; bright yellow throat, rump, and sides; white wing patch; blackish streaks on white sides; female—brownish-gray; yellow throat, rump, and sides
Length: 5.5" Weight: 0.43 oz Wingspan: 9.25"

Widespread and common throughout North America, the yellow-rumped warbler is a versatile and successful member of the avian world. The yellow-rumped warbler has two distinct subspecies. The somewhat duller "myrtle" warbler inhabits eastern North America; the brighter "Audubon's" warbler is found in the West. In winter they trade their bright summer feathers for a duller and less-conspicuous streaky brown molt. These small birds play an important role in maintaining insect populations, as they thrive on ants, grasshoppers, and gnats as well as spiders. They also eat spruce budworms, which are major defoliators of firs and spruce trees. Several other warblers to watch for are black-throated gray (*Dendroica nigrescens*), hermit (*D. occidentalis*), Townsend's (*D. townsendi*), and MacGillivray's (*Oporornis tolmiei*) warblers.

YELLOW WARBLER
Setophaga petechia
Wood warbler family (Parulidae)
Quick ID: yellow overall; yellow spots in tail; conspicuous black eye; male—reddish streaks on breast; female—duller yellow, lacks reddish streaks
Length: 5" Weight: 0.33 oz Wingspan: 8"

Due to their small size and often fleeting glimpses, warblers are often a challenge to identify. Many warblers have some yellow feathers, but fortunately the yellow warbler is quite easy to identify—it is the only warbler that is totally yellow. Wilson's warbler (*Wilsonia pusilla*) is yellow below but greenish yellow above, and the males have a small black cap and lack tail spots. Lesser goldfinches (*Carduelis psaltria*) are also mostly yellow but have blackish wings, and the males have a black cap. Orange-crowned warblers (*Vermivora celata*) are dusky yellowish green; while Nashville warblers (*V. ruficapilla*) have a gray head with white eye ring. Common yellowthroats (*Geothlypis trichas*) are dusky-brownish; males have a black mask.

SOOTY GROUSE
Dendragapus fuliginosus
Upland game bird family (Phasianidae)
Quick ID: chicken-like; mottled brownish-gray; long neck; long square tail; male has yellow combs over eye and yellow air sack on each side of neck surrounded by white feathers
Length: 20" Weight: 2.3 lb Wingspan: 26"

As taxonomists study and review new DNA evidence, historical classification schemes are being revised at a rapid rate. As recently as 2006, the blue grouse that roams the pine forests of western states was technically split by the taxonomists into two species. The sooty grouse found in the coastal western states is darker than the dusky grouse (*D. obscurus*), which is generally found in the Rockies. Highly camouflaged, the sooty grouse fades into obscurity in the pine forests of Yosemite. They spend much of their day walking under or near the cover of underbrush, hunting for insects and vegetation. In spring the males inflate their yellow neck sacs to call for females and establish territory.

PILEATED WOODPECKER
Dryocopus pileatus
Woodpecker family (Picidae)
Quick ID: large black body; white wing patch; white line on neck; large red crest on head; male—red forehead, red line behind bill; female—gray forehead, black line behind bill
Length: 16.5" Weight: 10 oz Wingspan: 29"

Pileated (pronounced "PILL-ee-ay-tid" or "PIE-lee-ay-tid") woodpeckers are strikingly large, crow-size birds that, when seen in their strong and direct flight, have a distinguishing large white patch in their wings. As they search for ants, the loud drumming of their bills on tree trunks can be distinctly heard as they carve out rectangular feeding holes. When building a nest cavity, they excavate holes 8 inches wide and from 10 inches to 2 feet deep in dead tree trunks. The word *pileated* means having a cap, or pileus. Look for pileated woodpeckers in Mariposa Grove and Yosemite Valley.

ACORN WOODPECKER
Melanerpes formicivorus
Woodpecker family (Picidae)
Quick ID: clown-like facial pattern; white breast with black streaks; solid black back; red crown (females have less red); white around forehead and throat; white eye; white patch in wing
Length: 9" Weight: 2.8 oz Wingspan: 17.5"

Many birds are named for their coloration or to honor an important scientist, but the acorn woodpecker is so named because it is so intertwined with its food source. Ranging from western Oregon to Mexico, these woodpeckers are easily recognized by their clown-like facial mask and raucous waca-waca call. Unlike most other woodpeckers, these fascinating birds live in social groups. They spend their days busily gathering acorns and wedging them into previously drilled holes in tree trunks, telephone poles, or other wooden structures. One such storage tree, called a granary, can hold thousands of acorns. The birds also eat insects, fruit, and sap. Found in oak woodlands, acorn woodpeckers may be spotted in Foresta, Cooks Meadow, and Yosemite Village.

GREAT GRAY OWL
Strix nebulosa
Owl family (Strigidae)
Quick ID: very large; mottled gray; rounded head without ear tufts; ring of concentric feathers surrounding each eye
Length: 27" Weight: 2.4 lb Wingspan: 52"

As the evening sun slides behind the granite peaks of Yosemite, moonlit shadows come alive with the sounds of creatures of the night. If you find a sheltered spot and sit quietly, you may be rewarded with a series of deep baritone hoos of a great gray owl. With a wingspan approaching 60 inches, the great gray is the largest owl in North America. Studies of great gray owl populations have revealed that these Sierra Nevada owls are a distinct subspecies. Other owls found in the park include the great horned owl (*Bubo virginianus*), which sports distinctive ear tufts, and the smaller spotted owl (*S. occidentalis*), which is spotted overall.

WRENTIT
Chamaea fasciata
Old World babbler family (Timaliidae)
Quick ID: grayish-brown; salmon-brown wash underneath; long tail; white eyes; small bill
Length: 6.5" Weight: 0.49 oz Wingspan: 7"

Difficult to see, the dull-colored wrentit makes up for its drab appearance with its peppy bouncing Ping-Pong-ball song of pip-pip-pipipipipi and rattling churr calls. Cocking its tail up and down, this small bird may pop out briefly for a look at you but then quickly dart back under cover. This bird is neither a wren nor a chickadee (in the Old World chickadees are called "tits"). Although inconclusive, DNA evidence has led researchers to believe that the wrentit is closely related to a family of birds normally found in Southeast Asia called Old World babblers. The smaller, more slender bushtit (*Psaltriparus minimus*) often travels in flocks and is not as secretive as the wrentit.

ANNA'S HUMMINGBIRD
Calypte anna
Hummingbird family (Trochilidae)
Quick ID: emerald green above, mottled grayish underparts; male—rosy pink head and throat and small white spot behind eye; female—pink patch under throat, indistinct white above eye
Length: 4" Weight: 0.15 oz Wingspan: 5.25"

In early spring, tiny flying sprites called Anna's hummingbirds begin actively building a tiny nest composed of soft cottonwood seed fluff bound together with sticky spiderwebs. Hatching from jellybean-size eggs, the young hummingbirds are fed a diet of insects until they can forage for sweet nectar on their own. Long flexible bills allow hummingbirds to probe into tubular flowers for the sugar-filled nectar. Also nesting in the park, the even tinier Calliope hummingbird (*Selasphorus calliope*) has a green back and mixed green, white, and pale rufous (rusty) underparts. Calliope males sport a stunning rosy-streaked gorget (throat feathers); the female has grayish streaks. Rufous hummingbirds (*S. rufus*) arrive later in the summer and have noticeable rufous-colored sides.

WESTERN BLUEBIRD
Sialia mexicana
Thrush family (Turdidae)
Quick ID: Male—shiny bright blue above; head and throat blue; chestnut-orange on sides, breast, and upper back; female—dull grayish blue; dull rusty underparts and back
Length: 7" Weight: 1 oz Wingspan: 13.5"

One of the most beloved of all birds, these avian beauties are also a great study subject for beginning birders to start noticing subtle differences in several species of birds that are adorned with blue feathers. Male western bluebirds have blue throats, while eastern bluebirds (*S. sialis*), which are found east of the Rockies, have orange feathers under their throat. Mountain bluebirds (*S. currucoides*), which are found at higher elevations, have no orange feathers at all. Female bluebirds are duller overall; the young are spotted. Steller's jays (*Cyanocitta stelleri*), which have a crest, and western scrub jays (*Aphelocoma californica*) also have blue feathers but are both much larger than bluebirds.

AMERICAN ROBIN
Turdus migratorius
Thrush family (Turdidae)
Quick ID: large songbird; upperparts gray to black; breast and underparts reddish orange
Length: 10" Weight: 2.7 oz Wingspan: 17"

One of the most familiar of all North American songbirds, the American robin is a member of the thrush family along with western bluebirds (*Sialia mexicana),* hermit thrushes (*Catharus guttatus*), and Townsend's solitaires (*Myadestes townsendi*). Robins have a characteristic habit of running a bit and stopping to search for insects and other invertebrates and then running a bit again. Hermit thrushes are smaller than robins, have a streaked breast, and are brown with a reddish tail. Townsend's solitaires are about the size of a robin but are gray and have a white ring around their eye and white outer tail feathers.

BLACK PHOEBE
Sayornis nigricans
Tyrant flycatcher family (Tyrannidae)
Quick ID: grayish-black with white belly; thin pointed bill; dark eye; wags tail
Length: 7" Weight: 0.67 oz Wingspan: 11"

The black phoebe is a shy but inquisitive bird that is very aware of your presence, usually before you are aware of this small bird. True to their name, black phoebes are grayish black all over except for a white belly that is conspicuous when seen from below. This flycatcher typically perches on a low branch, wagging its tail; when an insect is spied, it quickly darts out and catches the insect in midair before returning to its original perch. Other flycatchers in the park include olive-sided (*Contopus cooperi*), Hammond's (*Empidonax hammondii*), dusky (*E. oberholseri*), Pacific-slope (*E. difficilis*), and ash-throated (*Myiarchus cinerascens*). Look for black phoebes in wooded areas around Yosemite Falls, the Ahwahnee Hotel, and especially trails near water.

SIERRAN TREEFROG
Pseudacris sierra
Treefrog family (Hylidae)
Quick ID: slim waist; large head and eyes; round pads on toes; wide dark stripe through eye from mouth to shoulders; usually Y-shaped mark between eyes; extremely variable color from green, gray, brown, tan, reddish, or creamy; underside creamy; yellow under back legs
Length: 0.75–2"

One of the most common species of frogs in Yosemite, the tiny Sierran treefrog can be found at all elevations throughout the park. Their ribbit-ribbit chorus fills the air with spring song from ponds and meadows in an age-old landscape choir. As well as being extremely variable in coloration, these treefrogs have the ability to change quickly from dark to light to blend in with the background. The Sierran treefrog has recently been elevated to species status after being taxonomically split from the Pacific treefrog (*P. regilla*).

AMERICAN BULLFROG
Lithobates catesbeianus
True frog family (Ranidae)
Quick ID: large frog; green with or without gray or brown markings; eardrum larger than eye
Length: 3.6–8"

The American bullfrog is the largest frog in the United States and is native to the eastern states. Since its introduction into the West, it has thrived and become a major predator of fish, insects, small mammals, birds, and other amphibians. Resistant to a pathogenic chytrid fungus they carry, bullfrogs have a huge impact on native wildlife. Park biologists are taking steps to prevent annihilation of protected species that may be affected by these predatory frogs. Many species of amphibians are in severe decline, including the Sierra Nevada yellow-legged frog (*Rana sierrae*). As well as being extremely vulnerable to the chytrid fungus, this once-abundant frog is heavily preyed upon by introduced nonnative trout species.

SIERRA NEWT
Taricha sierrae
Newts and true salamander family (Salamandridae)
Quick ID: stocky, medium-size; yellowish brown above, orange below; bulging eyes
Length: 4.9–7.8"

Unique in the salamander world, newts undergo three distinct life cycles. They begin life in freshwater ponds as tadpoles. After several weeks they metamorphose into a land stage. During this juvenile stage, they leave their watery home and walk into the forest. Endemic to California, the Sierra newt is found along an area that passes through Yosemite National Park along the western slope of the Sierra Nevada. Their rough skin contains a powerful neurotoxin called tetrodotoxin, and their bright red-orange coloration serves to warn predators of their toxicity.

SIERRA ALLIGATOR LIZARD
Elgaria coerulea palmeri
Alligator lizard family (Anguidae)
Quick ID: large triangular head; long tail; olive-brown to blue-green with dark mottling; underside greenish-yellow; keeled scales
Length: 7–13.6"

Resembling a miniature alligator, the Sierra alligator lizard is one of twenty-two species of reptiles that can be found in Yosemite. The western pond turtle is the lone turtle, while six other lizards, including the San Diego alligator lizard (*E. multicarinata webbii*) are found here. The similar but smaller California whiptail (*Cnemidophorus tigris mundus*) is about 13 inches long and is slimmer, with a long slender tail. The tail of these lizards is easily broken off but gradually grows back. No lizards in Yosemite are venomous.

SIERRA MOUNTAIN KINGSNAKE
Lampropeltis zonata multicincta
Colubrid family (Colubridae)
Quick ID: red, black, and whitish alternating rings; smooth shiny scales
Length: 24–47"

Not all creatures that slither about and wait undercover in hiding are dangerous to humans. Of the thirteen species of snakes that can be found in Yosemite, twelve of them are nonvenomous to humans. Although the colorful black, white, and red rings of the Sierra mountain kingsnake resemble the venomous coral snake, this beauty is nonvenomous. These snakes are at home in wooded areas, where they hunt for small mammals and even other, smaller snakes.

SIERRA FENCE LIZARD
Sceloporus occidentalis taylori
Spiny lizard family (Phrynosomatidae)
Quick ID: medium-small; grayish-brown and black markings; keeled scales; male—blue on throat and sides of belly; female—few or no blue markings, dark bars and crescents on back
Length: 2.25–3.5"

With fresh air, rocky granite boulders, and gorgeous mountain scenery as their fitness center, Sierra fence lizards practice pushups and sprints on a daily basis. They are commonly seen sunning on rocks and fence posts, where males will often push up with their front legs to flash their shiny blue bellies before dashing to safety. Victims of frequent tick bites, these lizards do sustain tick populations, including blacklegged ticks, but a protein in their blood kills the bacterium *Borrelia burgdorferi* that these ticks spread, which causes Lyme disease.

NORTHERN PACIFIC RATTLESNAKE
Crotalus oreganus oreganus
Pit viper family (Viperidae)
Quick ID: brownish-gray; triangular head with vertical pupils; tail rattles (venomous!)
Length: 2–4'

The Northern Pacific rattlesnake is the only venomous snake in Yosemite. The triangular head and vertical pupils identify this snake as one of the pit vipers. Their cryptic patterns and coloration help conceal them as they hunt for rodents, insects, and other small reptiles and amphibians. The Pacific gopher snake (*Pituophis catenifer*), which looks somewhat like the rattlesnake, will shake its tail in dried leaves to resemble the rattle of the rattlesnake.

RAINBOW TROUT
Oncorhynchus mykiss
Trout family (Salmonidae)
Quick ID: olive-green; small, blackish spots on sides and fins; pinkish stripe on sides and cheeks
Length: 10–16" Weight: 2–6 lb

Named for the colorful pinkish stripe on its sides, the rainbow trout is originally native to the lower elevations of Yosemite. Only a handful of fish are native to Yosemite's waters, including the rainbow trout, California roach (*Hesperoleucus symmetricus*), Sacramento sucker (*Catostomus occidentalis*), and riffle sculpin (*Cottus gulosus*).

BROWN TROUT
Salmo trutta
Trout Family (Salmonidae)
Quick ID: black spots; red spots with blue halos; unspotted tail
Length: 10–16" Weight: 1–2 lb

Native to Europe, brown trout, or brownies as they are commonly called, were introduced into the West for sportfishing. These voracious predators compete with other fish, and declines in native trout species are common where these fish are found. Secretive, they favor areas with overhanging vegetation, undercut banks, and submerged snags and rocks. You may see these trout in Tuolumne Meadows streams.

EASTERN BROOK TROUT
Salvelinus fontinalis
Trout family (Salmonidae)
Quick ID: dark olive-green to brown; cream wavy lines (vermiculations) on back and head; sides with pale spots and red spots with bluish halos; bottom fins white-edged
Length: 5–20"   Weight: 2.2–13.2 lb

Yosemite's glacially carved lakes and cool high-altitude mountain streams were cut off from fish migration by waterfalls and steep mountainsides. In the late 1800s anglers began stocking fish into the high mountain streams and lakes, unaware of future ecological impacts. Stocking no longer occurs in the park, but introduced fish such as the brook trout still are found in many of the park's waters. Fishing regulations in Yosemite are available at www.nps.gov/yose/naturescience/upload/Fishing-Regulations.pdf.

Key Features of Trout

Trout Species	Description
Rainbow	Small, dense, black spots from tail to top of head with none on gill covers
Brown	Large, dense, black and red spots from tail to head with some on gill covers
Brook	Red spots with blue halos on sides as well as light spots (spots on top side are wavy); fins edged with white

SIERRA PERICOPID
Gnophaela latipennis
Erebid moth family (Erebidae)
Quick ID: medium-size; wings black with white markings
Wingspan: 0.98–1.18"
Flight Season: June–August

If you spot the slow, lazy flight of a black-and-white butterfly, you may actually have found Sierra pericopid, a day-flying moth. At rest, butterflies usually keep their wings folded up, while moths usually have their wings flat down. Often seen flying in summer is another day-flying moth called the red-shouldered ctenucha moth, *Ctenucha rubroscapus,* which gains protections from predators by its resemblance to a bumblebee or wasp (see inset).

SANDHILL SKIPPER
Polites sabuleti
Skipper family (Hesperiidae)
Quick ID: small, stocky body; variable orangish-yellow with dark markings
Wingspan: 0.87–1.25"
Flight Season: June–August

Small and mostly brown, skippers are often unnoticed and unappreci-ated members of the butterfly world. Nevertheless, for those who love butterflies, skippers are an exciting challenge to identify. Skippers make up about one-third of all the butterfly species in North America. With their stocky body, they look like a moth, but at rest they hold their wings up more like a butterfly.

LUSTROUS COPPER
Lycaena cupreus
Gossamer-wing butterfly family (Lycaenidae)
Quick ID: small; bright reddish-orange; upper wings edged with black, black spots; underwings grayish tinged with orange and black markings
Wingspan: 1.12–1.25"
Flight Season: June–August

Although small, the brightly colored cop-pers are sure to attract attention as they feed on nectar in flower-filled mountain meadows. The bright shimmer on the wings of the lustrous copper no doubt gave rise to its common name.

ACMON BLUE
Plebejus acmon
Gossamer-wing butterfly family (Lycaenidae)
Quick ID: bottom of wings white with black spots and orange markings; male—top of wings blue with dark border; female—top of wings brownish with orange band
Wingspan: 0.75–1.12"
Flight Season: March–October

These lovely little butterflies called "blues" are fun to watch as they collect nectar from spring and summer flowers. Yosemite is well known in the butterfly world for having a large number of species of blues and coppers. They sometimes sun themselves with wings open, revealing the various shades of blue. The underside of their wings is typically grayish with distinguishing markings. One of the most common of these butterflies, the Acmon blue, lays its eggs on buckwheats and lupines.

SIERRA NEVADA BLUE
Plebejus podarce
Gossamer-wing butterfly family (Lycaenidae)
Quick ID: male—silvery blue above; female—brown above, no orange below
Wingspan: 0.87–1.0"
Flight Season: June–September

No better match between a flower and a butterfly can be found than that of the dainty Sierra Nevada blue butterfly and its host plant, the graceful nodding magenta blooms of shooting stars (*Dodecatheon*). This species was first identified in Yosemite's high mountain meadows. Several closely related species reach far into the Arctic region.

CALIFORNIA HAIRSTREAK

Satyrium californica
Gossamer-wing butterfly
family (Lycaenidae)
Quick ID: upper side brown; orange
spots on hindwings; small hairlike tail
from each hindwing
Wingspan: 1.0–1.25"
Flight Season: May–August

Hairstreaks are small butterflies with threadlike or hairlike projections from their hind wings. The tails distract predators away from the vulnerable head. Many hairstreaks, including the California hairstreak, are attracted to fragrant blooms of dogbane, buckwheat, and buckeye.

CALIFORNIA SISTER

Adelpha californica
Brush-footed butterfly
family (Nymphalidae)
Quick ID: medium-size; brownish-
black; conspicuous white stripe on
upper wings, orange blotch near
wing tips; underside with brownish,
orange, white, and bluish markings
Wingspan: 2.5–4"
Flight Season: March–October

The prominent white stripes on the wings of this group of butterflies earned them the name "sisters," as they somewhat resemble the crisp white lines of a nun's habit. The caterpillars eat the leaves of oak trees, which can be found at lower and mid elevations. The California sister is similar in appearance to Lorquin's admiral (*Limenitis lorquini*), but its larval food plants include willows and poplars, which can be found at higher elevations in the park.

MONARCH
Danaus plexippus
Brushfoot family
(Nymphalidae)
Quick ID: orange with black veins;
white spots on black wing borders
Wingspan: 3.5–4"
Flight Season: April–November

One of the most well-known
members of the insect world,
the monarch easily lives up to its celebrity status. The yellow-and-black-
striped caterpillars feed on plants in the milkweed family, ingesting
toxins that render them distasteful to predators. Carrying these toxins into adulthood, the orange-and-black coloration warning is recognized by predators and confers parallel protection to other, similarly
colored butterflies.

VARIABLE CHECKERSPOT
Euphydryas chalcedona
Brushfoot family
(Nymphalidae)
Quick ID: medium-size; forewings long
oval-shaped, brownish-black to orang-
ish with variable white, orange, and
reddish checkers; underside paler
Wingspan: 1.25–2.25"
Flight Season: April–July

The striking white, red, yellow, to orange patterns on the variable
checkerspot are truly eye-catching. The females lay their eggs on penstemons, paintbrushes, and snowberry.

HOARY COMMA
Polygonia gracilis
Brushfoot family (Nymphalidae)
Quick ID: scalloped wings; orange with black and yellow markings, dark border; underside mottled brown, gray, and white with small silvery-white C-shaped mark
Wingspan: 1.5–2.25"
Flight Season: June–September

Also known as anglewings, this group of butterflies is named for a small silvery-white C-shaped mark on the underside of their mottled-brown wings. Caterpillar host plants include currants and gooseberries (*Ribes sp.*) and western azalea (*Rhododendron occidentale*).

76

HYDASPE FRITILLARY
Speyeria hydaspe
Brushfoot family (Nymphalidae)
Quick ID: medium to large; reddish orange–brown with black and silver spots
Wingspan: 2.0–2.5"
Flight Season: June–September

The rusty colored fritillaries are often difficult to distinguish among species. Some, such as the Hydaspe and Zerene fritillaries (*S. zerene*), are placed in a group of medium-size "frits" called greater fritillaries. The caterpillars feed on violets.

WESTERN TIGER SWALLOWTAIL
Papilio rutulus
Parnassian and swallowtail family (Papilionidae)
Quick ID: large; yellow with black stripes; one tail on each hindwing
Wingspan: 2.75–4"
Flight Season: June–July

One of the most familiar butterflies, the western tiger swallowtail delights butterfly lovers throughout most of the western states. The very similar two-tailed swallowtail (*P. multicaudata*) has narrower tiger stripes and two hairlike tails.

CLODIUS PARNASSIAN

Parnassius clodius

Parnassian and swallowtail family (Papilionidae)

Quick ID: fairly large; white with blackish markings; male—two small red spots; female—three small red spots

Wingspan: 2–2.6"

Flight Season: June–July

Parnassian refers to Mount Parnassus in Greece, which was sacred to Apollo, and these butterflies are sometimes called Apollo butterflies. After mating, the male clodius Parnassian places a waxy plug on the tip of the female's abdomen to prevent other males from mating with her. Flying at the highest altitudes in the park, the Sierra Nevada Parnassian (*P. behrii*) has yellowish-orange spots.

SARA ORANGETIP
Anthocharis sara
White and sulphur family
(Pieridae)
Quick ID: medium-size; white; orange
wingtips edged with black
Wingspan: 1.06–1.6"
Flight Season: May–June

Also known as the Pacific
orangetip, the Sara oran-
getip has white wings with
orange tips. Look for this graceful butterfly in the foothills of the park
and the similar and just as attractive Stella orangetip (*A. stella*) at higher
elevations.

SIERRA SULPHUR
Colias behrii
White and sulphur family
(Pieridae)
Quick ID: green above and below;
male—yellow-fringed wings; female—
pink-fringed wings
Wingspan: 1.37–1.62"
Flight Season: July–August

A widespread genus, sulphurs are usually white or yellow. Also known
as the Sierra green sulphur, the Sierra sulphur is the only sulphur in
its range that is greenish. It is endemic to the high elevations of the
Sierra Nevada.

WHITE-LINED SPHINX

Hyles lineata
Sphinx moth and hawkmoth family (Sphingidae)
Quick ID: heavy-bodied; olive-brown; black wings with pink and white markings beat rapidly to hover
Wingspan: 2.43–3.56"
Flight Season: February–November

The white-lined sphinx moth is often mistaken for a small hummingbird or a bumblebee and is commonly known as a hummingbird moth. You can sometimes spot them at dusk, when they uncurl their long, needlelike mouthpart called a proboscis to sip nectar from flowers.

INYO GRASSHOPPER
Trimerotropis inyo
Short-horned grasshopper
family (Acrididae)
Quick ID: small; dark bands on gray
body; short antennae
Length: 1.2–1.6"

This small grasshopper makes
its home in the steep and rocky
high-elevation habitats on the
eastern slopes of the Sierra
Nevada. The blotchy Inyo grasshopper is highly camouflaged against its
rocky granite home east of Tioga Pass.

YELLOW-FACED BUMBLEBEE
Bombus vosnesenskii
Bee family (Apidae)
Quick ID: black; yellow face; yellow abdomen
stripe; large yellow patch at top of back; hairy
black hairs on underside of abdomen
Length: up to 0.55"

The yellow-faced bumblebee is found
only in West Coast states, including
California. Bumblebees are important
pollinators, especially at high altitudes,
such as those found in Yosemite.

BEE FLY
Bombylius sp.
Bee fly family (Bombyliidae)
Quick ID: small; yellow with black patches and stripes; large eyes; long dark legs; long proboscis
Length: 0.55–0.71"

Members of the bee fly family look like bees, but they lack stingers. This adaptation may offer these flies some protection from predators reluctant to fight what they think are stinging prey. Some bee flies have extremely long proboscises, which they plunge into the depths of tubular flowers to reach the nectar.

WHITE-SPOTTED SAWYER
Monochamus scutellatus
Longhorned beetle family (Cerambycidae)
Quick ID: shiny black body; very long black-and-white antennae; white spot between body and head; female—mottled white spots
Length: 0.7–1.0"

The white-spotted sawyer is a native wood-boring insect that is found in coniferous forests. Its larvae develop in diseased and damaged conifers and help break down the wood fibers, adding nutrients back into the soil.

CALIFORNIA PRIONUS
Prionus californicus
Longhorn beetle family
(Cerambycidae)
Quick ID: reddish brown; smooth shiny wings
Length: 0.9–2.2"

No friend of orchardists, the California prionus is a member of the longhorn beetle family that spends most of its life underground as a fleshy grub. It dines on tree, shrub, and vine roots, sometimes killing the plant.

COBALT MILKWEED BEETLE
Chrysochus cobaltinus
Leaf beetle family
(Chrysomelidae)
Quick ID: small, oval; metallic greenish blue; clubbed antennae
Length: 0.24–0.35"

Summer visitors to Yosemite Valley may notice tiny sparkling jewels adorning the leaves of milkweed plants. Cobalt milkweed beetles lay their eggs on milkweed; after hatching, the ravenous larvae eat away the leaves, leaving only the skeletonized veins.

CONVERGENT LADY BEETLE
Hippodamia convergens
Ladybird beetle family (Coccinellidae)
Quick ID: oval dome-shaped; red with 12 black spots
Length: 0.16–0.2"

Of the more than 400 species of lady beetles in North America, the convergent lady beetle is one of the most common. Appreciated by gardeners, lady beetles readily dine on aphids, which are tiny insects that suck juices from plants.

GIANT GREEN WATER BEETLE
Dytiscus marginicollis
Predaceous diving beetle family (Dytiscidae)
Quick ID: large aquatic beetle; oval shape narrows to points at ends; black to reddish brown, often with greenish sheen
Length: 1–1.3"

Patrolling small ponds for a quick meal, predaceous diving beetles send other water creatures scurrying for cover. Even the long slender larvae, called water tigers, prey on many insects.

MONO LAKE ALKALI FLY

Ephydra hians
Shore fly family
(Ephydridae)
Quick ID: tiny; dark brown with
bluish-green metallic shine
Length: 0.16–0.27"

Of the 1,500 species of tiny shore flies, those that thrive in the alkaline waters of nearby Mono Lake, just to the east of Yosemite, may be the most famous flies in the world. As masses of shorebirds feast on these brine flies, birders arrive from around the world to see the show.

WESTERN BLACK-LEGGED TICK

Ixodes pacificus
Hard tick family (Ixodidae)
Quick ID: small oval, flat body; 8 black legs
and back plate; male—blackish abdomen;
female—reddish abdomen; larva—smaller,
with 6 legs
Length: 0.1–0.2"

Some western black-legged ticks carry the spiral-shaped bacterium that causes Lyme disease. Ticks wait patiently on a blade of grass or shrub until a host such as a lizard, mammal, or human passes by and then grab on for a ride.

EMERALD SPREADWING
Lestes dryas
Spreadwing family (Lestidae)
Quick ID: male—metallic green, blue eyes; female—brownish, brown eyes
Length: 1.4–1.6"

Damselflies have long slender bodies and hold their wings above their bodies when perched. The related dragonflies have long stout bodies and when perched extend their wings to each side. The emerald spreadwing may rest with its wings partially open.

TWELVE-SPOTTED SKIMMER
Libellula pulchella
Skimmer family (Libellulidae)
Quick ID: brown with yellow side stripe; male—12 brown wing spots and 8 white wing spots; female—12 brown wing spots but no white wing spots
Length: 1.9–2.0"

Dragonfly fossils date back about 325 million years. Dragonflies have stout long bodies, and when perched they extend their wings to each side. The long body and clasping "tail" of dragonflies cause some people to falsely believe they have stingers. Males and females can vary greatly in size and coloration. Look for dragonflies such as the twelve-spotted skimmer along streams and ponds.

SMALL MILKWEED BUG
Lygaeus kalmii
Seed bug family (Lygaeidae)
Quick ID: grayish-black; orange-red–lined partial hourglass patterned on back; several small white spots on upper end of hind parts rimmed with white
Length: 0.4–0.5"

The brightly colored small milkweed bug stands out as it forages on plants, including milkweeds. Milkweeds contain toxins called cardiac glycosides that can affect heart rate. These beetles can absorb the toxin without ill effect, and their aposematic (warning) colors alert would-be predators.

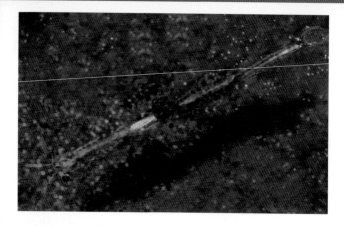

SPINYTAIL FAIRY SHRIMP
Streptocephalus sealii
Fairy shrimp family (Streptocephalidae)
Quick ID: tiny, aquatic, clear; multiple pairs of swimming legs
Length: 0.24–0.98"

Fairy shrimp are tiny aquatic arthropods in the same group of animals as crabs, lobsters, and shrimp. You can see spinytail fairy shrimp swimming in May Lake. Outside the eastern side of Yosemite, the Mono Lake brine shrimp (*Artemia monica*) are an important source of food for birds.

GOLDENROD CRAB SPIDER
Misumena vatia
Crab spider family
(Thomisidae)
Quick ID: crab-like legs; flattened body; female—white to yellow with red band on sides; male—darker reddish-brown, whitish body with brownish marks; first two pairs of legs reddish-brown, last two pairs yellowish
Length: 0.12–0.35"

Resembling tiny crabs, these flower spiders sit motionless on flowers, waiting for passing prey insects such as bees, wasps, and flies. One of the few spider species capable of changing colors, after several days they gradually assume the color of their surrounding flower heads. Their larger relatives, black widow spiders and tarantulas, are also found in the park.

GIANT WESTERN CRANE FLY
Holorusia hespera
Large crane fly family (Tipulidae)
Quick ID: long thin brown to reddish-brown body; 6 long spindly legs, black "knees"; 2 delicate paddle-shaped wings, about 3–5" across
Length: body 1.6–2.0"

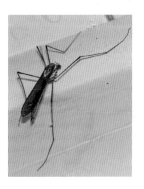

If you see an insect that resembles a giant mosquito or flying spider as big as a child's hand, it is most likely an innocent giant western crane fly. As startling as they first appear, adult crane flies are totally harmless and somewhat fragile, as their legs break off easily. Erroneously called mosquito hawks, most adults are only interested in mating and do not eat at all.

CADDISFLY
Genus and species vary
Various families (Order: Trichoptera)
Quick ID: dull brownish to yellowish; moth-like; two pairs of wings with small hairs; wings held tent-like; long antennae
Length: body about 1" (varies)

Of the more than 1,100 species of caddisflies in the United States, 199 are found in the Sierra Nevada; of those, thirty-seven species are endemic. Anglers study the minute details as they prepare their flies to grab the attention of trout. The aquatic worm-like larvae build a protective case made of stones, twigs, or leaves.

WHITE ALDER
Alnus rhombifolia
Birch family (Betulaceae)
Quick ID: pale green 3" egg-shaped leaves, finely toothed;
male flowers on 0.4–0.8" long narrow drooping cylinders
(catkins); female flowers become small woody cone-like
structures that enclose seeds; grayish-white bark
Height: 50–80'

Named for its pale green leaves, white alder typically flowers from January into April, producing
flowers on drooping spikes of catkins. Common in Yosemite Valley, white
alder sometimes forms large thickets. It is found mainly near streams and
open moist areas. Alders are able to tolerate poor soil conditions due
to nitrogen-fixing bacteria found in the root nodules, which add valu-
able nitrogen back into the ecosystem. The winged seeds of alders are
enclosed in small woody, cone-like structures that may remain on the tree
for a year. Also found in Yosemite Valley and sequoia groves, hazelnut
(*Corylus cornuta*) has similar leaves and shape but has hairy woody fruits
that appear to have the shape of a bird's beak.

MOUNTAIN DOGWOOD
Cornus nuttallii
Dogwood family (Cornaceae)
Quick ID: rounded top; low spreading branches; tiny greenish-yellow flowers, 6 white petal-like bracts about 5" across; red oval fruit; opposite elliptical leaves with veins that curve toward the tip; bark reddish brown
Height: 10–40'

Heralding the arrival of spring, mountain dogwoods glow brightly against the waking forests. The jovial white blossoms are made up of large overlapping bracts that surround the tiny greenish-yellow flower center. In fall the showy auburn leaves add color to the forest, and the reddish fruits are sought after by birds including band-tailed pigeons and pileated woodpeckers. The fine-grained hardwood of mountain dogwood has been used to make tools, cabinets, piano keys, golf club heads, and bows and arrows. The young shoots were used in basket making. Look for mountain dogwood in Wawona and Yosemite Valley.

INCENSE CEDAR
Calocedrus decurrens
Redwood or cypress family (Cupressaceae)
Quick ID: overlapping scalelike leaves; twigs flattened, fanlike; reddish-brown cones, 0.75–1", scales in 3 parts; bark cinnamon-red irregular ridges with flattened platelike scales
Height: 70–120'

Outcompeted by e-technology, the humble pencil still has its place in the world of communication. The source of most #2 pencils in the United States is the incense cedar, a tree that is native to California, Oregon, and Nevada. The aromatic wood is also prized for its durability, as it resists rotting and is used for fence posts, lumber, and cedar chests. If you look closely at this tree, the branchlets look like small flat fans, which have been resourcefully used as whiskbrooms. American Indians used the leaves to treat stomach problems and colds. Incense cedar is a common component of oak woodland forests, including those in Yosemite Valley.

WESTERN SIERRA JUNIPER
Juniperus occidentalis
Cypress family (Cupressaceae)
Quick ID: evergreen; rounded crown; grayish-green leaves, flattened and scalelike, covered in resin; small round fruits, 0.25" in diameter, bluish-green when young, turning blue-black when mature; bark shreddy and reddish brown
Height: 15–30'

Often called Sierra juniper, the western juniper is an evergreen that is easily identified by its flat scalelike leaves, peeling reddish-brown bark, and round berrylike fruits. When rubbed the leaves smell like gin. The small round fruits are pale bluish-green when young with a whitish waxy coating; after about 2 years they mature, turning blue-black. The seeds provide an important source of nutrition for birds, including jays, robins, and woodpeckers. Another juniper can be found in the park at high altitudes, such as those at Tioga Pass. Dwarf juniper (*J. communis*) is a short plant, only up to waist high, with sharp-pointed leaves in whorls of three forming wide prostrate shrubs.

GIANT SEQUOIA
Sequoiadendron giganteum
Redwood or cypress family (Cupressaceae)
Quick ID: massive, open-spreading crown; alternate bluish-green needlelike leaves, 0.25",
overlapping; cinnamon-red deeply furrowed bark; trunk 10–20' in diameter; woody
cones 0.5–2.5", scales thickened at end
Height: 150–275'

Towering above all other trees in Yosemite, the giant sequoia is one of
nature's grandest members, some individuals reaching 275 feet into the
sky. Protected within the boundaries of Yosemite are three groves of these
massive trees, including the Tuolumne and Merced Groves and the larger
Mariposa Grove, with about 500 mature sequoias. Coast redwoods beat
out sequoias in record heights, and bristlecone pines are the oldest, but
sequoias have the largest volume. Measuring 34,005 cubic feet in volume,
Yosemite's Grizzly Giant is the largest sequoia in the park. Just south in
Sequoia National Park, the General Sherman tree tops the list at 52,508
cubic feet and is big enough to hold nearly 400,000 gallons of water.

CANYON LIVE OAK
Quercus chrysolepis
Beech family (Fagaceae)
Quick ID: dense rounded crowns; short crooked trunks; branching limbs; sharp-tipped alternate evergreen leaves, elliptical, 1–4", toothed or smooth; egg-shaped acorns with hairy golden brown caps; rough gray bark
Height: 20–65'

Unlike most oaks, canyon live oak and its relatives have thick glossy evergreen leaves that remain on the tree. With leaves that somewhat resemble those of hollies, the upper surface is dark green, while the lower surface is grayish to yellowish green. Commonly known as golden cup oak, its acorn caps are golden brown with yellowish fuzz. After preparing the acorns, American Indians used the meal to make flour for bread. Early settlers used the strong wood to make wagon wheels and wedges. In the foothill regions, the similar interior live oak (*Q. wislizenii*) has long narrow acorns that lack the golden wooly caps. Look for canyon live oak in Wawona and the Merced River Canyon.

CALIFORNIA BLACK OAK
Quercus kelloggii
Beech family (Fagaceae)
Quick ID: deciduous; spreading branches; rounded crown; shiny green leaves, 5–7 deep lobes with bristle tipped teeth; acorns 1–1.5" with deep scaly caps; bark in small plates
Height: 30–80'

Probably no other tree has played such an important role in the lives of animals and people in Yosemite as the California black oak. Wildlife such as black bears, mule deer, squirrels, and acorn woodpeckers all depend on the acorns for nourishment. American Indians also used black oak acorns as an important food source. Dried acorns were pounded with rocks into flour and used as a staple meal. In autumn the leaves turn yellowish orange, which glows brilliantly in the sunlight. Look for California black oaks throughout Yosemite Valley, especially in Cooks Meadow. Yosemite holds several other species of oaks, including a shrub called huckleberry oak (*Q. vaccinifolia*), which can be seen at Glacier Point and along Tioga Road.

CALIFORNIA BUCKEYE
Aesculus californica
Horse chestnut family (Hippocastanaceae)
Quick ID: deciduous, opposite finely toothed leaves in 5 parts looks like a palm with 5 fat spreading fingers; pinkish-white flowers in 4–8" long upright clusters; fruit a pear-shaped leathery brown capsule with seams
Height: 12–30'

Found in the foothills at low elevations in the park, California buckeye is a small tree or branching shrub with numerous spreading branches and rounded crown. Flowering in May and June, the sweet smelling pinkish-tinged white flowers adorn upright clusters that attract butterflies such as azures and blues. The five-part leaves drop off the tree in late summer, leaving the pear-shaped fruits hanging from the branches. Inside the leathery husk, the large glossy brown seed somewhat resembles the eye of a deer, prompting the common name, buckeye. The bark, leaves, and fruit contain a toxin called aesculin, and the seeds were used to stupefy fish in streams. Today aesculin is used in labs to identify species of bacteria.

CALIFORNIA BAY LAUREL
Umbellularia californica
Laurel family (Lauraceae)
Quick ID: 3–5"-long oblong shiny evergreen leaves with smooth edges; small yellowish-white flowers; green turning bluish-black fruit (drupe) with yellowish stalk; short gray trunk with spreading branches
Height: 40–80'

The California bay laurel, or California bay, is a well-known tree or large shrub native to California and Oregon. American Indians used the aromatic leaves to cure headaches, but in some people they can cause headaches. The leaves were used to flavor foods and made into teas and infusions. They were also used to wash sores and used as an insecticide. The fruit, known as California bay nut, resembles a small avocado. After roasting, the large inner seeds were eaten or ground into meal. The highly prized light brown wood is used for making furniture, bowls, spoons, and guitars. California bay laurel is one of the hosts for the fungal-like pathogen *Phytophthora ramorum*, which causes sudden oak death (SOD).

RED FIR
Abies magnifica
Pine family (Pinaceae)
Quick ID: evergreen; upward curved flat needles about 1" long, 4-angled with a ridge on top with bluish-white covering; cylindrical upright cones 6–9"; deeply ridged reddish-brown bark
Height: 150–180'

Two species of fir can be found in Yosemite: white fir (*A. concolor*), starting at mostly lower elevations, and red fir, reaching into higher elevations. Firs are typically soft to the touch (think of soft animal fur), while spruces are sharp and will stick you. Spruces also leave a prominent woody peg on the stem when a needle falls off. An individual spruce needle has four sides and easily rolls in your fingers, while a fir needle is flat and flops over when you try to roll it. White fir can be found at Glacier Point; California red fir, with its distinctive red bark, can be seen at Crane Flat and along Tioga Road.

WHITEBARK PINE
Pinus albicaulis
Pine family (Pinaceae)

Quick ID: evergreen; high elevations only; short crooked trunk with irregular spreading crown; needles 1.5–2.75", dull green with faint white lines in bundles of 5 crowded at the end of twigs; cones 1.5–3.25", rounded thick scales with sharp edge; thin whitish-gray scaly bark

Height: 20–50'

Exposed to the harsh conditions of the high-altitude environment, the whitebark pine grows in Yosemite's subalpine zone to timberline. At the tree line, some of these pines grow in a low stunted form known as *krummholz*, a German word meaning "crooked wood." Whitebark pines are a primitive group of pines known as stone pines due to their wingless seeds. Fortunately for this tree, Clark's nutcrackers prefer these seeds and break open the cones with their strong beaks to reach the seeds. In the process, some seeds are dropped and forgotten and eventually sprout into seedlings. Populations of this unique tree are in serious decline due to attacks by white pine blister rust and mountain pine beetles.

LODGEPOLE PINE
Pinus contorta
Pine family (Pinaceae)
Quick ID: 1–3" needles in bundles of 2, sharply pointed and often twisted; 2" cones with raised rounded scales and sharp points, many remaining closed for years; bark thin, flaky, and scaly
Height: 50–80'

Found in thick stands, the tall, slender lodgepole pines are found in the park from about 6,500 to 9,800 feet elevation and are the most wide-spread tree in Yosemite. The strong, straight trunks were once used as building poles for American Indian tepees. Adapted to forest fires, the cones often remain on the trees for many years until high heat from a forest fire causes them to open and drop their tightly held seeds to the ground, where they can sprout to regenerate the forest. This type of heat-exposed seed-release cone is called a serotinous cone. Needle miner moths and pine beetles cause defoliation and eventual death of lodgepole pines.

JEFFREY PINE
Pinus jeffreyi
Pine family (Pinaceae)
Quick ID: evergreen; 5–11" needles in bundles of 3, dull dark blue-green, often twisted; cones 5–9", egg-shaped with inward curving prickles; cinnamon-red bark with broad scaly plates
Height: 60–170'

Similar in appearance to the more common Ponderosa pine (*P. ponderosa*), Jeffrey pine is found in open flat areas, such as granitic domes, at higher elevations than Ponderosa pine. The bark of Jeffrey pine has a fruity vanilla-pineapple smell, while that of Ponderosa pine has a resinous odor. Due to the shape of the prickles, the cones of Ponderosa pine feel sharp to the touch, while those of Jeffrey pine generally do not. The tree was named to honor nineteenth-century Scottish botanist John Jeffrey (1826–54). A particular Jeffrey pine on Sentinel Dome was made famous in a striking photo by Ansel Adams.

SUGAR PINE
Pinus lambertiana
Pine family (Pinaceae)
Quick ID: evergreen; branches perpendicular to trunk; bark deep reddish with deep fur-rowed ridges; blue-green needles with white lines, 2.75–4", in clusters of 5; cones very long, 10–23", without prickles
Height: 100–210'

A giant among its cousins, the sugar pine is the largest species of pine tree, approaching the giant sequoia in total volume. The massive cones of sugar pines are what most people notice first, as they range from 10 to 23 inches long. Pines have two types of cones. Male cones are small and often hang in long, soft clusters. The female cones are the ones we usually associate with conifers. They start out green and sticky then, after windborne fertilization, harden into brown cones to protect the seeds inside the scales. Pine seeds, or pine nuts, are high in protein, fat, and many vitamins and minerals. They are enjoyed by squirrels, birds, and also by people.

FOOTHILL OR GRAY PINE

Pinus sabiniana
Pine family (Pinaceae)
Quick ID: grayish-brown bark with ridges and large scales; needles grayish-green, 7.8–11.8", in clusters of 3; dense large egg-shaped cones, 6–10", with downward prickles
Height: 40–80'

When trying to determine the species of pines, one of the most important characteristics to note is the number of needles that are bunched together. In gray or foothill pine, there are three needles per bundle. Found at lower elevations in Yosemite, this pine is also characterized by its distinctive grayish-green needles and grayish bark that leads to another common name of ghost pine. The cones are stout and heavily armored with curved 1-inch hooks. California Indians ate the seeds fresh or dried them for winter use. The long needles were used for bedding and floor coverings, and the root fibers were used to make baskets. The pitch was applied to burns and sores and also used as glue.

DOUGLAS-FIR
Pseudotsuga menziesii
Pine family (Pinaceae)
Quick ID: pyramidal shape with long drooping branches; green needles, 1", flat soft and fragrant, spreading in 2 rows; cones 2–3.5" with 3-pointed bract that hangs downward; reddish-brown-gray bark, thick and furrowed
Height: 80–120'

The name of this evergreen tree is misleading, as the Douglas-fir is not a fir at all but more closely related to hemlocks. The hyphen in the name indicates that it is not a true fir. It was named for Scottish botanist David Douglas (1798–1834). In Yosemite it grows on moist forested slopes in Yosemite Valley, Hetch Hetchy, and Wawona. The unique three-pointed bracts that stick out of the cones are helpful in distinguishing this tree from other conifers. Mice, chipmunks, and squirrels eat the seeds of Douglas-firs. American Indians used the wood for baskets and lumber and steeped the needles into a medicinal tea.

MOUNTAIN HEMLOCK
Tsuga mertensiana
Pine family (Pinaceae)
Quick ID: evergreen; pyramid-shaped; top tends to bend over; short 0.5–0.75" single needles, spirally arranged; small woody 1–3" cones
Height: 30–100'

Gracing the high mountain slopes year-round with its soft branches, the mountain hemlock is a beauty among trees. Mountain hemlocks frame the shoreline around Tenaya Lake and other high elevations along Tioga Road. Snow slides off the drooping branches, making mountain hemlock one of the few trees that can withstand heavy snowfall without broken branches. The top branches of mountain hemlock can be a good way to identify this tree, as they are often gracefully bent over.

QUAKING ASPEN
Populus tremuloides
Willow family (Salicaceae)
Quick ID: broad 1–3" deciduous leaves, heart-shaped to round with finely toothed margins; flowers 1–3" catkins; bark smooth whitish-gray, often with dark scars
Height: 40–75'

The leaves of quaking aspen top flattened, thin, flexible stems that quiver kite-like with the slightest breeze. In autumn the yellow leaves paint golden ribbons along streambeds and open areas in the park. Genetically identical to the parent tree, aspens produce shoots that grow into clones, with many members sharing the same root system. Aspen clones spread over 100 acres, and all the trees are considered one plant. Look for quaking aspen along Tioga Road and at higher elevations in the park. In the same genus, black cottonwood (*P. balsamifera* ssp. *trichocarpa*) is common in Yosemite Valley; Fremont cottonwood (*P. fremontii*) is found at low elevations near El Portal.

BIGLEAF MAPLE
Acer macrophyllum
Soapberry family (Sapindaceae)

Quick ID: large, branching, rounded crown; large leaves opposite with 5 deep, long pointed lobes; fruits double samaras with wings; bark with furrows in 4-sided plates

Height: 40–100'

With leaves as large as a dinner plate, this is one plant that lives up to its name. Found from Alaska to California, bigleaf maple has the largest leaves of any maple, some leaves approaching nearly 1 foot across. Deer often browse the young saplings. In fall the leaves turn yellow, adding to the brilliance of autumn in the park. Look for bigleaf maple in Yosemite Valley, especially along Bridalveil Creek. A small, shrubby tree with slender branches and smaller leaves, mountain, or Torrey, maple (*Acer glabrum* var. *torreyi*) is the other species of maple in the park. The subspecies of mountain maple in the park is named for American botanist John Torrey (1796–1873).

CALIFORNIA NUTMEG
Torreya californica
Yew family (Taxaceae)
Quick ID: evergreen; alternate needlelike leaves 0.9–2.7" long; light brown bark with scaly ridges; olive-like fruit, 1–1.4", yellowish-green with purple streaks
Height: 15-79'

Endemic to California, the California nutmeg is named for the resemblance of its fruit to that of the unrelated spice. Inside the olive-like fruit is a single astringent seed, the white part of which is edible. When crushed the needles emit a pungent odor, leading to the common name stinking cedar. Also called California Torreya, the genus name *Torreya* honors American botanist John Torrey (1796–1873), who made significant contributions to the botanical records of the United States. This tree often grows along steep, rocky, usually south-facing slopes in partial shade or full sun. California nutmeg can be found in Hetch Hetchy, along Big Oak Flat Road, and in the Mariposa Grove.

BLUE ELDERBERRY
Sambucus nigra ssp. *cerulea*
Elderberry family (Adoxaceae)
Quick ID: white flowers in flat sprays; leaves with 5–9 finely toothed leaflets; berries blue with whitish coating
Height: 6.5–26'

Three species of elderberries are found in Yosemite, including blue elderberry, which has a powdery coating on its blue berries. The tart berries have long been gathered for use in making jellies, pies, and wine. Black elderberry (*S. melanocarpa*) has dark blue berries; red elderberry (*S. racemosa*) has toxic red berries.

SKUNKBUSH SUMAC
Rhus trilobata
Cashew family (Anacardiaceae)
Quick ID: yellow flowers on small spikes appear before the leaves; 3 alternate scalloped leaflets; fruit a reddish berrylike drupe
Height: 2.6–4.6'

Similar in appearance to the leaves of poison oak (*Toxicodendron diversilobum*), skunkbush sumac leaves have an unpleasant odor when crushed. The sour but edible berries have been used to make a refreshing lemonade-like drink. American Indians used the bark and stems to make baskets.

WESTERN POISON OAK
Toxicodendron diversilobum
Cashew family (Anacardiaceae)
Quick ID: erect shrub or vine-like; bright green shiny leaves with 3 toothed leaflets, 0.7–2.8", turning red in fall; white berries
Height: 3.4–9.8'

Many people experience itchy contact dermatitis after exposure to this shrub, and visitors to Yosemite would be well advised to learn to identify poison oak, as it differs in form and appearance from the vine-like characteristics of its eastern relative, poison ivy (*T. radicans*). Western poison oak is typically an erect shrub with gangly branches and lobed, shiny green leaves.

MOUNTAIN BIG SAGEBRUSH
Artemisia tridentata ssp. *vaseyana*
Aster family (Asteraceae)
Quick ID: evergreen; greenish-silver hairy leaves with 3 blunt teeth; creamy yellow flowers on narrow stalks
Height: 6–12'

A widespread shrub of western states, sagebrush is a member of the aster family but lacks the showy flowers of most asters. Found along the Tioga Road and Mono Pass, the outer tip of the leaves of mountain big sagebrush are divided into three lobes, hence the species name *tridentata*, which means "three-toothed." The pungent odor of sagebrush is derived from volatile oils that help protect the plant from insects and browsing by wildlife. In fall the bitter compounds break down and the numerous seed heads provide food for wildlife. Found in Yosemite Valley, another sagebrush relative, mugwort (*A. douglasiana*), was used by American Indians to treat poison oak rashes.

BLOOMER'S GOLDENBUSH
Ericameria bloomeri
Aster family (Asteraceae)
Quick ID: broad compact; leaves narrow, linear; yellow raggedy flowers in dense clusters
Height: 8–23"

Bloomer's goldenbush often grows in dry, rocky places and can be found along Tioga Road and Crane Flat. A common name that is often given to this and other look-alikes is rabbitbrush, as small mammals such as rabbits seek shelter under them. The small seeds are attached to a tuft of fine hair that is easily dispersed by the wind.

YERBA SANTA
Eriodictyon californicum
Borage family (Boraginaceae)
Quick ID: shredding bark; alternate, evergreen leathery lance-shaped leaves, shiny green on top, underside with matted hairs; small funnel-shaped lavender flowers
Height: 2–8'

The aromatic leaves of this shrub have long been prized for their varied medicinal uses, so much so that the early Spanish settlers named it sacred or holy herb—yerba santa. The leaves and flowers were made into a tea used for coughs, colds, and rheumatism. A poultice of pounded leaves was applied to sores and wounds.

CALIFORNIA SPICEBUSH
Calycanthus occidentalis
Strawberry shrub family (Calycanthaceae)
Quick ID: rounded, leathery oval opposite glossy leaves; leathery maroon-red flowers with strap-like petals
Height: 4–12'

The leathery, maroon-red flowers of California spicebush are from 2 to 4 inches across. The petals and sepals look alike, which botanists then call tepals. This shrub can be seen in Yosemite Valley around the lodges and campgrounds. American Indians scraped the bark and used it medicinally to treat colds and sore throats.

PURPLE-FLOWERED HONEYSUCKLE
Lonicera conjugialis
Honeysuckle family (Caprifoliaceae)
Quick ID: opposite elliptical 1–3" leaves; paired dark purplish-red tubular flowers, 0.25–0.5"; fruit paired reddish-orange berries
Height: 2–6'

With more than 200 species in this genus of honeysuckles, the vine forms are typically called honeysuckles and many of the shrubs are commonly called twinberries. Purple-flowered honeysuckle, also called double honeysuckle or twinberry, has both the flowers and fruits joined like twins. Another twinberry with similar growth habits, *L. involucrate*, has yellow flowers.

MOUNTAIN SNOWBERRY
Symphoricarpos rotundifolius var. *rotundifolius*
Honeysuckle family (Caprifoliaceae)
Quick ID: opposite oval leaves with wavy edges; light pink bell-shaped flowers; fruit a white berrylike drupe; hairy twigs
Height: 1–3'

Found in dry areas around Tuolumne Meadows, mountain, or round-leaf, snowberry is sometimes known as waxberry. By September unusual (and toxic) white berrylike fruits called drupes replace the pale pink bell-shaped flowers.

MARIPOSA MANZANITA
Arctostaphylos viscida ssp. *mariposa*
Heath family (Ericaceae)
Quick ID: reddish-brown peeling bark; small whitish to pinkish urn-shaped flowers;
berrylike fruits
Height: 3–13'

Several species of manzanita are found in Yosemite. Pinemat manzanita
(*A. nevadensis*) forms sprawling mats in forests along Tioga Road.
Greenleaf manzanita (*A. patula*) is an erect shrub with glossy leaves
forming extensive stands in montane areas. Two subspecies of whiteleaf
manzanita are found in Yosemite: mariposa manzanita (*A. viscida* spp.
mariposa), which is common in Yosemite Valley, and whiteleaf manzanita
(*A. viscida* spp. *viscida*), which reaches lower elevations.

WESTERN AZALEA
Rhododendron occidentale
Heath family (Ericaceae)
Quick ID: smooth alternate 1–4" leaves; large white trumpet-shaped flowers with yellow splotches; 5 long stamens
Height: 3–10'

Native to California, the western azalea is a large showy shrub that fills the air with intoxicating fragrance. In June and July masses of white trumpet-shaped flowers greet visitors to Cook's Meadow in Yosemite Valley.

DWARF BILBERRY
Vaccinium cespitosum
Heath family (Ericaceae)
Quick ID: alternate oval 2" leaves; pink bell-shaped flowers; blue berries
Height: 2–4"

This shrub goes by many common names, including dwarf blueberry, bilberry, and huckleberry. The oval leaves are about 2 inches long, with tiny teeth on the margins. The branches are round; the roots are fibrous and form low spreading shrubs that are especially numerous in timberline regions. You can find dwarf bilberry in high mountain meadows such as Tuolumne Meadows. Western, or bog, blueberry (*V. uliginosum* ssp. *occidentale*) is a low shrub about 2 feet tall that forms thickets in similar habitats, such as along Glacier Point Road.

WESTERN REDBUD
Cercis occidentalis
Pea family (Fabaceae)
Quick ID: rounded crown; alternate round 1–4" leaves heart-shaped at base; fruits flat, leathery 2–4" pods that hang in clusters
Height: 8–20'

Spring comes early to the low elevations of Yosemite, heralded by the blossoms of western redbud. Often in full bloom by the end of March, the magenta-pink flowers appear before the leaves are fully formed. The blooms are edible and make a nice addition to spring salads. Along with deer brush (*Ceanothus integerrimus*) and buck brush (*C. cuneatus*), the twigs of redbud were used to make baskets and cradles.

BUSH CHINQUAPIN
Chrysolepis sempervirens
Beech family (Fagaceae)
Quick ID: evergreen; oblong 1.5–3" leaves, smooth green on top, underneath rusty-golden, slightly hairy; white flowers in spikes; nuts in hard spiny case
Height: 1–6'

The long leathery leaves with rusty hairs underneath are characteristic of bush chinquapin. The edible light brown nuts are enclosed in a spiny burr-like case. Look for this shrub at Crane Flat and Glacier Point.

HUCKLEBERRY OAK
Quercus vacciniifolia
Beech family (Fagaceae)
Quick ID: large dense shrub; evergreen leaves, oval, usually smooth edged but may have teeth
Height: 1–4'

Forming dense stands of shrubs, this oak does not resemble its relatives. Huckleberry oak is quite different in appearance from the stately California black (*Q. kelloggii*), canyon live (*Q. chrysolepis*), and interior live (*Q. wislizenii*) oaks that are found in the park. Mule deer browse on the leaves and twigs of this shrub, and in fall the acorns are eaten by black bear, quail, and other animals. Huckleberry oak is commonly found in Yosemite Valley, along Tioga Road, and at Glacier Point and may be one of the first plants to develop after fires.

SIERRA GOOSEBERRY
Ribes roezlii
Currant family (Grossulariaceae)
Quick ID: spreading branches, leaves with 3–5 lobes; purplish-red flowers; round reddish spiny berry
Height: 1–3'

Eight species of gooseberries or currants can be found in Yosemite, several of which grow only in the subalpine or alpine regions. The Sierra gooseberry is common throughout Yosemite Valley and in the giant sequoia groves. American Indians ground gooseberries to eliminate the stickers on the fruits before eating them.

DEER BRUSH
Ceanothus integerrimus
Buckthorn family (Rhamnaceae)
Quick ID: large bushy shrub lacking thorns; elliptical leaves; tiny white flowers in long fragrant 2.5–6" clusters
Height: 3–12'

This group of shrubs called ceanothus often sport stunning floral displays of creamy white to blue flowers in spring. Deer brush and buck brush (*C. cuneatus*) are two of the taller eight ceanothus species found in Yosemite; others, such as Fresno mat (*C. fresnensis*), form low prostrate mats.

UTAH SERVICEBERRY
Amelanchier utahensis
Rose family (Rosaceae)
Quick ID: diverging branches; oval toothed, slightly hairy leaves; loose 5-petaled white flowers; fruit bluish-black, berrylike (pome); reddish-brown to grayish bark
Height: 3–15'

The white flowers of Utah serviceberry adorn this shrub in April through June. It is an important food plant for mule deer and birds. The berrylike fruits typically stay on the branches until they are eaten.

BIRCH-LEAF MOUNTAIN MAHOGANY
Cercocarpus betuloides
Rose family (Rosaceae)
Quick ID: evergreen, alternate leaves, 0.5–1", oval, finely toothed, woolly white below, wedge shaped at base; bark gray squares
Height: 5–12'

Birch-leaf mountain mahogany is a large shrub or small tree that grows in dry areas of the foothills and lower elevations. The conspicuous fruits have 2- to 3-inch long feathery bundles of whitish streamers.

MOUNTAIN MISERY
Chamaebatia foliolosa
Rose family (Rosaceae)
Quick ID: alternate fernlike evergreen leaves; flowers with 5 white petals
Height: 7.8–23.6"

Mountain misery is a small shrub that forms dense low carpets under tall pines. It is especially prevalent along the road in the Wawona area and near Foresta. Unlike its sweet-smelling relatives, this member of the rose family got its name from its burning tar–like aroma. It also exudes a gummy resin that sticks to hands, clothes, and shoes. The resin makes the shrub highly flammable.

THIMBLEBERRY
Rubus parviflorus
Rose family (Rosaceae)
Quick ID: leaves with 5 sharply toothed lobes; gray-brown peeling bark; stems with hairy glands but no prickles; white flowers with 5 petals and yellow-tipped stamens form ring in the center; wide red thimble-shaped fruit
Height: 3–6'

The leaves of thimbleberry look like large soft maple leaves, but the white flowers resemble those of a wild rose. The red fruits can be eaten raw or used to make jams and jellies.

131

CALIFORNIA MOUNTAIN ASH
Sorbus californica
Rose family (Rosaceae)
Quick ID: leaves with 7–11 finely toothed oval leaflets; fruit red, berrylike pome; tiny white flowers in clusters
Height: 3–9'

The many branching arms of California mountain ash may be overlooked much of the year, but in fall the bright red berrylike pomes draw attention to this shrub.

SIERRA WILLOW
Salix eastwoodiae
Willow family (Salicaceae)
Quick ID: wooly branches; elliptical leaves with hairs on both sides, becoming smooth with age; flowers in 1.2–2.4" catkins
Height: 2–19'

About 400 species of willows are found in North America; hybrids occur frequently, making identification a notorious challenge. Willows range in size from tall trees to ankle-high shrubs. At high elevations like Tuolumne Meadows, willows such as the Sierra or mountain willow and gray-leaved Sierra willow (*S. orestera*) often have protective hairs on the leaves.

TWINING BRODIAEA
Dichelostemma volubile
Asparagus family (Asparagaceae)
Quick ID: long twining stem, rose-pink sphere of flowers at end; long straight 1–2.5'
leaves with parallel veins

Flowering from May through July the rose-purple flowers of twining brodiaea, or twining snake lily, may ramble for 2 to 5 feet with a rose-pink
ball of flowers at the end. Endemic to California, twining brodiaea can
be found at the lower elevations in the western end of Yosemite, where
it grows in open areas and meadow edges. The common name brodiaea
honors Scottish botanist James Brodie (1744–1824). Not a true vine, it
has recently been moved from the Lily family to the Asparagus family. In
the same genus, blue dicks (*D. capitatum*) is a common early-spring
bloomer with lovely violet flowers atop a long spindly stem.

CALIFORNIA MANROOT
Marah fabacea
Gourd family (Cucurbitaceae)
Quick ID: waxy white star-shaped flower; climbing stem with branching tendrils; broad leaves with 5 pointed lobes on stem; round green to yellow fruits with prickles

The stout 4- to 20-foot stems of California manroot arise from a very large thick underground taproot. In the foothills from April through June, small waxy white flowers appear on the vine and then are replaced by a prickly round green fruit. All parts of the plant are bitter and poisonous, and the spines on the fruit can irritate the skin. The seeds inside the fruit were ground and mixed with skunk grease as an early baldness preventive. The other species of manroot in the park, *M. horridus*, has deeply cut leaves and oval fruits with stiff spines.

COW PARSNIP

Heracleum sphondylium ssp. *montanum*
Carrot family (Apiaceae)

Quick ID: large 4–8" flat clusters of small white flowers; maple-like leaves up to 12"; very tall grooved, hairy stem

Height: 3–10'   Bloom Season: May–July

Towering above the other flowers in Cook's Meadow, the white dinner plate–size flowers of cow parsnip sway gently in the summer breezes. With leaves up to 12 inches across, the genus name *Heracleum* appropriately honors Heracles (Hercules), son of Zeus. American Indians peeled the tender young stalks and boiled them in stews. Children used the hollow stems as blowguns and flutes. A poultice of mashed roots was applied to sores and bruises. The roots have been shown to have medicinal properties and are currently being tested. Older field guides may list various Latin names for cow parsnip, as the scientific name was recently changed from *H. lanatum* and *H. maximum* to *H. sphondylium*.

RANGER'S BUTTONS
Sphenosciadium capitellatum
Carrot family (Apiaceae)
Quick ID: white round button-size flower heads; long broad leaves highly divided; flower stems densely hairy; flat fruits
Height: 1.5–6' Bloom Season: July–August

Ranger's buttons grow in moist meadows, along waterways, and in high rocky areas in the park. The balls of white flowers appear as small pompoms raised high like troops of happy cheerleaders. Known by many common names, such as swamp white heads, woollyhead parsnip, and button parsley, this plant has toxic properties that made it useful as a wash to repel lice. Ranger's buttons are similar in appearance to several other tall white plants, including Brewer's angelica (*Angelica breweri*) and cow parsnip (*Heracleum sphondylium* ssp. *montanum*), but the flowers of ranger's buttons are in distinctive rounded balls rather than flattened bundles.

SHOWY MILKWEED
Asclepias speciosa
Dogbane family (Apocynaceae)
Quick ID: pompom-like heads of starlike pink flowers; oval leaves with velvety white hairs
Height: 1–4' Bloom Season: May–July

Of the four species of milkweed found in the park, showy milkweed is the one that is commonly seen in Yosemite Valley and throughout the mixed conifer forests. Even though milkweeds are poisonous, many parts of the plant were traditionally used for medicinal purposes. The milky latex in the stems and leaves was used to remove warts, corns, and calluses. Monarch butterflies lay their eggs on the underside of milkweed leaves. When the caterpillars emerge, they feed on the toxic leaves, incorporating the toxins into their bodies, the taste of which deters predators such as birds. Also look for orange-and-black small milkweed bugs (*Lygaeus kalmii*) and cobalt milkweed beetles (*Chrysochus cobaltinus*) on the flowers.

BIGELOW'S SNEEZEWEED
Helenium bigelovii
Aster family (Asteraceae)
Quick ID: outer ray flowers yellow, reflexed downward with ends lobed; dome-shaped inner disk flowers yellow to purplish-brown; clasping, linear smooth-edged leaves
Height: 1–3' Bloom Season: June–September

Sneezeweed is a plant in the aster family with showy outer ray flowers and inner disk flowers that produce pollen. Bigelow's sneezeweed was named to honor Dr. John Milton Bigelow (1804–78), a physician and botanist from Ohio who collected plants and took part in the Pacific Railroad Survey of 1853–54 to determine the best route for the transcontinental railroad. The plant was used medicinally as a snuff ingredient that when inhaled induced a sneeze, driving evil spirits and sickness out of the body. Look for Bigelow's sneezeweed in Yosemite Valley, Wawona, and the Glacier Point area, including McGurk Meadow.

CALIFORNIA CONEFLOWER
Rudbeckia californica
Aster family (Asteraceae)
Quick ID: hairy stem; leaves lance-shaped to elliptical; ray flowers yellow, reflexed downward; disk flowers greenish-yellow and raised on a 1–2" column
Height: 2–6' Bloom Season: July–August

A California native, the California coneflower is easily recognized by its raised cone-shaped center that holds the disk flowers. This striking yellow coneflower was named to honor the father-son team of Olaf Rudbeck Sr. (1630–1702) and Olaus Rudbeck Jr. (1660–1740), who were professors at Uppsala University in Sweden. Another member of this genus, Black-eyed Susan (*R. hirta* var. *pulcherrima*) now grows in Yosemite Valley after being introduced from the East. In July fields of California coneflower can be seen in Crane Flat, Mariposa Grove, and Wawona.

WESTERN WALLFLOWER
Erysimum capitatum
Mustard family (Brassicaceae)
Quick ID: orange or yellow clusters of flowers, 4 opposite petals; thin flat seedpods
Height: 1–2' Bloom Season: June–August

Decorating roadsides and dry open areas, the orange and yellow flowers of western wallflower brightly bloom through early summer. A member of the mustard family, the plant's flowers each have four petals forming a cross, which is typical of mustards. A species of wallflower in Europe grows on vertical stone fences and walls, earning the common name wallflower, which has continued to be used for its ground-loving North American relatives. Wallflowers are found throughout Yosemite, with plants with yellow flowers typical at higher elevations and those with orange flowers at low elevations. Wallflowers are commonly seen along Glacier Point Road.

PINEDROPS
Pterospora andromedea
Heath family (Ericaceae)
Quick ID: tall reddish-brown stem; pale yellow urn-shaped flowers
Height: 1–4' Bloom Season: June–August

Oddities among the wildflower world, pinedrops frequently catch the eye of hikers in rich woodlands. Even though the plant can reach 4 feet tall, the reddish-brown stem blends well with the dappled forest light, making them difficult to see. Tiny yellow urn-shaped flowers hang down from the top of the stem, which is covered with a sticky substance. The stem becomes woody when dry and often remains standing throughout the winter season. Pinedrops lack chlorophyll and are reliant on the roots of conifers and a soil fungus to provide nourishment. Pinedrops may not bloom consistently, but look for them in rich woodlands, including areas such as Crane Flat, Ahwahnee, and Wawona.

SNOW PLANT
Sarcodes sanguinea
Heath family (Ericaceae)
Quick ID: red spike; tiny red waxy flowers with overlapping bracts; red scale-like leaves; turns black with age
Height: 6–11" Bloom Season: May–July

The snow plant is undoubtedly the most startling and unusual plant in Yosemite. Found only in California, Nevada, and Oregon, the bright red snow plant is the showstopper of the shaded forest floor. The snow plant lacks chlorophyll and thus cannot make its own food by photosynthesis. Instead it has established a relationship with a specific underground fungus (*Rhizopogon ellenae*) that in turn has a symbiotic relationship with the roots of mainly pine trees. Watch carefully and you may get to see a hummingbird sipping nectar from the flowers. Look for these unusual "fungus flowers," as they are sometimes called, in Wawona and Glacier Point.

143

LYALL'S LUPINE
Lupinus sellulus var. *lobbii*
Pea family (Fabaceae)
Quick ID: blue spikes of pea-like flowers; 5–7 leaflets on fan-shaped leaf, hairy
Height: 2–4" Bloom Season: July–August

Lupines (pronounced "LOO-pins") are a diverse group of wildflowers taking forms from just several inches tall, such as dwarf lupine (*L. nanus*), to shrub-size bush lupine (*L. albifrons*). Lyall's lupine is common in sub-alpine and alpine zones. Most lupines are blue, but the colors also vary greatly and can include yellow, purple, red, pink, and white. There are over twenty species of lupine in the park, with several subspecies. The blue flowers sometimes form large colonies, and it once was mistakenly thought that the plants robbed the soil of nutrients, which led to the name "lupine," which means wolflike or ravenous. Lupines have root nodules containing nitrogen-fixing bacteria that allow the plant to deposit nitrogen back into the soil.

HARLEQUIN LUPINE
Lupinus stiversii
Pea family (Fabaceae)
Quick ID: pink and yellow flowers; 6–8 slightly hairy wedge-shaped leaflets in fan shape
Height: 4–18"   Bloom Season: April–July

Of the over twenty species of lupines in Yosemite, harlequin lupine is undoubtedly the easiest to identify. Endemic to California, this lupine is a favorite of wildflower lovers and a visual treat for visitors to Yosemite. The upper petals, called banners, are bright yellow; the lateral petals, called wings, are bright pink. The first specimen collected was in 1862 by an army physician named Charles Stivers in Yosemite. Look for harlequin lupine in Yosemite Valley, Hetch Hetchy, and Wawona.

WESTERN BLUE FLAG
Iris missouriensis
Iris family (Iridaceae)
Quick ID: loose 3–4" lavender-blue flowers with yellow and purple marks; flexible 2–3'
sword-shaped leaves with parallel veins; slender stem with 1 to 3 flowers per stem
Height: 8–20" Bloom Season: May–June

Western blue flag is also known as Rocky Mountain iris and extends its
range from Southern California into Montana and Wyoming. Spring
flowers form dense lavender colonies in wet meadows such as those in
Yosemite Valley and Tuolumne Meadows. Three large sepals that resemble petals have purple and yellow markings that help guide pollinators
into the flower. The plant spreads by thick fibrous roots called rhizomes
and enjoys a rather untouched life, as the bitter leaves are shunned by
deer. The tough flexible leaves were used to make baskets, and fibers were
woven into ropes and cords. The slightly shorter Hartweg's or Sierra iris
(*I. hartwegii*) is found in drier, low elevations, such as near El Portal.

SUBALPINE MARIPOSA LILY
Calochortus leichtlinii
Lily family (Liliaceae)
Quick ID: bowl-shaped white flowers tinted smoky blue; petals have hairy triangular yellow bases with a deep maroon-red spot above; linear leaves at base often withered
Height: 8–24" Bloom Season: June–August

Subalpine mariposa lily is also known as smokey or Leichtlin's mariposa lily. Sometimes these members of the lily family are referred to as sego lilies or mariposa tulips due to their resemblance to tulips. The creamy white bowl-shaped petals resemble the wings of a butterfly, hence the name mariposa, which in Spanish means "butterfly." Four species of mariposa lilies can be found in the park. A species that occurs in Wawona, butterfly mariposa lily (*C. venustus*) may have variable salmon to yellowish colored petals. Subalpine mariposa lily is found in open, gravely areas in coniferous forests and along trails such as Lukens Lake and May Lake Trails.

SIERRA TIGER LILY
Lilium parvum
Lily family (Liliaceae)
Quick ID: as many as 40 orange horizontal or upturned bell-shaped flowers with purple spots, petals bend slightly backward at the tip; 1–6" lance-shaped leaves along stem or in whorls
Height: 2–6' Bloom Season: July–September

The elegant Sierra tiger lily is a native wildflower in the northern and central Sierra Nevada. Also known as alpine lily, it blooms in wet meadows, along creek sides, and in moist forests, including giant sequoia groves in the park. Hummingbirds as well as large butterflies including western tiger swallowtails (*Papilio rutulus*) and pale swallowtails (*P. eurymedon*) help pollinate the Sierra tiger lily. The Sierra tiger lily shares this genus in Yosemite with a large white lily called Washington lily (*L. washingtonianum*), named to honor Martha Washington, wife of the first US president, George Washington. Look for Sierra tiger lilies along Glacier Point Road and in the Wawona area.

NARROW PETALED TRILLIUM
Trillium angustipetalum
Bunchflower family (Melanthiaceae)
Quick ID: 3 long maroon upright petals, 3 sepals; 3 broad heart-shaped mottled leaves
Height: 8–27" Bloom Season: May–July

For wildflower lovers visiting Yosemite, the appearance of graceful blooms of narrow petaled trillium, or wake-robin, is one of nature's highlights. Beginning in May, this extraordinary wildflower unfurls its blossoms and leaves in multiples of three. The only trillium in the park and endemic to California, narrow petaled trillium, also called giant trillium, has thin maroon upright petals that blend surprisingly well with the surrounding forest. Look for trilliums near the Ahwahnee Hotel and along Wawona trails.

CORN LILY
Veratrum californicum
Bunchflower family (Melanthiaceae)
Quick ID: tall plant in wet meadows at mid to high altitude; alternate corn-like clasping 6–12" leaves; small white flowers with 6 petals
Height: 3–6' Bloom Season: July–August

Although this plant is known by many common names, including California corn lily, skunk cabbage, and false hellebore, by late summer the identification of this plant is unmistakable. Towering up to 6 feet tall in wet meadows, the dense flags of white flowers sit atop a tall corn-like stalk complete with long parallel veined leaves that clasp the stalk. Highly toxic, corn lily contains an alkaloid called cyclopamine that causes birth defects in animals such as sheep that eat the plant when pregnant. Cyclopamine inhibits a cell-signaling pathway called hedgehog and is being used in anti-cancer studies. You can spot corn lily in wet meadows, including those near May Lake, Crane Flat, Glacier Point, and Tuolumne Meadows.

PUSSYPAWS
Cistanthe umbellata
Montia family (Montiaceae)
Quick ID: rosette of spatula-shaped leaves flat on ground; reddish stems radiate from center; cat paw–like clusters of pale pink and white flowers
Height: 2–10" Bloom Season: May–August

Some plants are named for their identifying characteristics, and pussypaws could not have had a better common name. Lying flat on the ground in a wagon wheel shape, the flattened circle of flower balls resembles pink fuzzy cats' paws. This plant has recently undergone a taxonomic upheaval, with not only a genus change from *Calyptridium* to *Cistanthe* but also a family change from the Purslane family to the Montia, or miner's lettuce, family. *Cistanthe* is from the Greek words *kistos*, describing a plant called rockrose, and *anthos*, which means "flower."

FIREWEED
Epilobium angustifolium
Evening primrose family (Onagraceae)
Quick ID: spires of rose-pink flowers; alternate narrow leaves
Height: 2–6' Bloom Season: July–September

The stunning magenta flowers of fireweed line the roads in many areas of the park. Quickly colonizing burned areas, fireweed spreads rapidly, creating waving meadows of beauty where fire recently blackened the earth. The small seeds that are encased in erect, slim pods are attached to fluffy white hairs that sail the seeds through the air when the pods dry. Deer eat the flowers and stems. High in vitamins, the plants were also used as a nutritious food source by American Indians, who ate the young shoots like asparagus and enjoyed the flower petals steeped as a beverage. The species name comes from the Latin words *angustus*, which means "narrow," and *folium*, meaning "leaf."

MOUNTAIN LADY'S SLIPPER

Cypripedium montanum
Orchid family (Orchidaceae)
Quick ID: large white flower with purple markings and pouched lip; 2–6" narrow twisted purple sepals
Height: 8–28"   Bloom Season: May–July

Although humans are ineffective pollinators, along with insects we are drawn to the alluring sight and smell of orchids. Orchids make up one of the largest families of flowering plants in the world, with over 25,000 different species in 880 separate genera. Orchid enthusiasts delight in growing and propagating thousands of hybrids and cultivars. Wild orchids may not be faring so well. Misguided wildflower lovers attempt to transplant them, but orchids are so specific and bound to certain underground fungi that this attempt ends in failure. One of the twelve species of orchids in Yosemite, mountain lady's slipper has an inflated balloon-like pouch that resembles a bedroom slipper or moccasin.

SIERRA BOG ORCHID
Platanthera dilatata var. *leucostachys*
Orchid family (Orchidaceae)
Quick ID: spike of white flowers with long spurs; leaves alternately clasp the stem, narrow lance-shaped with parallel veins
Height: 6–52" Bloom Season: May–August

One of the most common of the dozen orchid species found in Yosemite, the Sierra bog orchid often occurs in extensive groups in bogs and wet meadows. Not all orchids have the large showy blooms typical of orchids sold in floral shops. The flowers of bog, rein, and ladies' tresses orchids grow along upright spikes that are easily overlooked. The similar green rein orchid (*P. sparsiflora*) has greenish flowers and is typically found at higher elevations in the park. In 2007 park biologists celebrated the description of a new species of orchid endemic to Yosemite called the Yosemite bog orchid (*P. yosemitensis*), which has yellowish flowers and an odor of stinky feet.

SUBALPINE PAINTBRUSH
Castilleja lemmonii
Broomrape family (Orobanchaceae)
Quick ID: pinkish-purple flowers; hairy stems and leaves
Height: 5–8"   Bloom Season: July–August

The colorful tubular leaves that at first glance appear to be the flowers hide the true flower of all paintbrushes. Over a dozen species of paintbrushes can be found in Yosemite in a rainbow of colors, with most orange, red, or purple, but yellow and cream colored flowers are also found. The showy colored parts of paintbrushes are actually leaflike bracts and sepals. The actual flower petals are fused into a narrow greenish-yellow tube. Subalpine, or Lemmon's, paintbrush grows in Tuolumne and Dana Meadows forming large masses of spectacular wildflowers. It also grows in the mountainous regions of California and a small portion of northern Nevada. The genus name *Castilleja* honors Spanish botanist Domingo Castillejo (1744–93).

STEER'S HEAD
Dicentra uniflora
Poppy family (Papaveraceae)
Quick ID: tiny white flowers with pink tinge that resemble a steer's head; leaves divided
Height: 1–4" Bloom Season: May–July

Some wildflower enthusiasts might overlook such a tiny flower as steer's head, but its uncanny resemblance to the head of a steer makes it worth the challenge to find. The tiny flowers seem to disappear into the rocky soils where they grow. It is often easier to first spot the separate, highly dissected green leaves and then look for the flower. Photographers will need to pull out the macro lens to get a close-up, as the whole flower is no larger than a quarter. Look for steer's head as the snow is melting in gravelly areas along Tioga Road.

CALIFORNIA POPPY
Eschscholzia californica
Poppy family (Papaveraceae)
Quick ID: bright orange bowl-shaped flower, 4 wedge-shaped petals with pink rim underneath; lacy leaves
Height: 8–24"   Bloom Season: March–June

The end of March finds many wildflower lovers and nature photographers heading to the hillsides at the foothill edges of the park. The show-stopping display of bright orange California poppies often joins forces with bright blue lupines, creating a bright palate of color. The California poppy is honored as the state flower of California. The very similar tufted poppy (*E. caespitosa*) is also found in the park, but it lacks the pink rim under the petals that the California poppy sports. Look for tufted poppy in open fields near Wawona.

LEWIS' MONKEYFLOWER
Mimulus lewisii
Lopseed family (Phrymaceae)
Quick ID: rose-pink flowers 1.25–2", 5 petals; finely toothed opposite oval leaves with sticky hairs
Height: 1–3' Bloom Season: June–September

You will have to come to California to see the beautiful Lewis' monkey-flower—it is found nowhere else. Monkeyflowers are so named because of the five petals that imaginatively resemble a monkey's face with broad jaws. Over twenty-five species of monkeyflowers can be found in Yosemite. Lewis' monkeyflower is widespread in wet meadows from 4,000 to 10,000 feet. Some species of monkeyflowers are pollinated by humming-birds, but Lewis' monkeyflower is pollinated by bees. It has two petals turned upward and three petals turned downward, with red-spotted yellow ridges leading into the mouth of the flower.

PRIDE OF THE MOUNTAIN
Penstemon newberryi var. *newberryi*
Plantain family (Plantaginaceae)
Quick ID: low stems in mats on rock; tubular magenta 1" flowers, upper lip has 2 lobes and lower lip has 3 lobes; leathery egg-shaped leaves
Height: 6–12"   Bloom Season: June–August

Stunning magenta masses of pride of the mountain, or mountain pride, flowers are a highlight of the natural rock gardens along the high winding vistas of Tioga Road. These high-elevation beauties rely on pollination from hummingbirds and bees during the short growing season. *Penstemons* are a large genus, with about 275 species in North America. The common name beardtongue comes from the hairy part inside the flower. The tubular or funnel-shaped flowers can range in color from blue to pink to red.

SCARLET GILIA
Ipomopsis aggregata
Phlox family (Polemoniaceae)

Quick ID: thin bright red trumpet-shaped 1" flowers with 5 pointed lobes; spindly, slightly hairy stems; narrow 1–2" finely dissected leaves

Height: 12–31"   Bloom Season: July–September

The striking 1- to 2-inch red tubular flowers of scarlet gilia are the perfect match for a hummingbird's long thin bill. Sometimes called skyrocket or fairy trumpet, scarlet gilia was once placed in the genus *Gilia* but later changed to *Ipomopsis*. The common name gilia (pronounced "GEE-lee-uh") honors Italian naturalist Filippo Luigi Gilii (1756–1821). When crushed, the leaves omit a skunk-like odor, prompting another common name: skunk flower. Look for scarlet gilia along Glacier Point and Tioga Roads.

SIERRA SHOOTING STAR
Primula jeffreyi
Primrose family (Primulaceae)
Quick ID: 4 bright magenta petals with maroonish-brown, white, and yellow at the center; tall spindly stems; strap-like leaves
Height: 6–23" Bloom Season: June–August

Also known as Jeffrey's shooting star, the Sierra shooting star lights up Yosemite's high-altitude meadows with its bright magenta petals. The petals of this unusual flower flare backward, looking somewhat like the trails left behind shooting stars. While Sierra shooting star is the most common shooting star in Yosemite, three other species can be found here. The alpine shooting star (*P. tetrandra*) blooms in the high altitudes in July and August. The subalpine shooting star (*P. subalpina*) is a small delicate flower endemic to the Sierra Nevada; it blooms from May to July, mostly in the southern part of the park. Henderson's shooting star (*P. hendersonii*) blooms from February to May at low elevations, including spectacular displays near El Portal.

CRIMSON COLUMBINE
Aquilegia formosa
Buttercup family (Ranunculaceae)
Quick ID: nodding red-and-yellow flowers with 5 upward-turned spurs; long slender stems; 3-lobed leaflets
Height: 1.5–3.5' Bloom Season: June–August

Blooming throughout Yosemite, crimson columbine is an eye-catching red-and-yellow flower. The spectacular nodding flower has five red backward-pointing spur-like petals with yellow borders. The tips of the pointed spurs contain nectar. Probing for the sweet treat, hummingbirds inadvertently pollinate the flower. The genus name *Aquilegia* comes from the Latin word aquila, which refers to an eagle's talons. At higher altitudes, the alpine columbine (*A. pubescens*) can be found sporting white flowers tinged with yellow and violet.

MARIPOSA RUSH
Juncus dubius
Rush family (Juncaceae)
Quick ID: heads in flat bottomed balls on stiff stems
Height: 6–27.5"

Sedges and rushes, very common and important members of the forest community, are often misidentified as grasses. Rushes have round stems, while the related sedges have edged stems. Mariposa rush, also known as questionable rush, was first discovered in Wawona Meadow. This species of rush is endemic to California.

163

BLUE-JOINT GRASS
Calamagrostis canadensis
Grass family (Poaceae)
Quick ID: clumps; slightly nodding branched purplish-blue heads; flat drooping leaves with rough hairs
Height: 2–4'

With over 10,000 species, the grass family is the fifth-largest family of plants. Grasses have jointed stems, while the stems of sedges and rushes lack joints. The stems of sedges have edges and those of rushes are round. Blue-joint grass is common and widespread over much of the United States and Canada. It grows shallow, spreading underground roots called rhizomes, sometimes so thick that they cause the underlying soil to decrease in temperature.

Quick ID for Grasses, Sedges, and Rushes

	Family	Stem
Grasses	Poaceae	Jointed, usually round
Sedges	Cyperaceae	Lacking joints, usually triangular
Rushes	Juncaceae	Lacking joints, rounded and solid

GIANT CHAIN FERN
Woodwardia fimbriata
Deer fern family
(Blechnaceae)
Quick ID: vase-like clumps of large fronds; evergreen
Height: 16–69"

Rising up from a single base, the great arching fronds of giant chain fern resemble a large green fountain. Most of the relatives of giant chain fern are found in the tropics. American Indians used the leaves to line cooking pits to bake acorn bread and other foods. Yosemite Falls Trail and Happy Isles are good places to see this fern.

BRACKEN FERN
Pteridium aquilinum
Bracken fern family
(Dennstaedtiaceae)
Quick ID: large long arching stem; leaves at end divided into 3 triangular parts
Height: 2–6'

Bracken fern does not grow in clusters as many other ferns do but is on individual upright stems and forms large colonies. Found on every continent except Antarctica, these ancient ferns have been found in the fossil record from over 55 million years ago. Along with grasses, willows, and sumacs, the dark underground roots (rhizomes) of bracken ferns were gathered in fall and processed to be woven into baskets.

SMOOTH SCOURING RUSH

Equisetum laevigatum
Horsetail family (Equisetaceae)
Quick ID: jointed stem with whorls of tiny scalelike leaves; spores in cone-like structure at tip of stem
Height: 12–31"

Resembling tall asparagus plants, scouring rushes, or horsetails, are ancient wetland plants, some of which grew to tree size proportions. Three species are found in Yosemite. Smooth scouring rush has joints with one ring of tiny leaves at the top of the joints; the very similar common scouring rush (*E. hyemale* ssp. *affine*) has rings of tiny leaves above and below the joint. Common horsetail (*E. arvense*) is shorter and has brush-like leaf stems.

LEATHERY GRAPE FERN
Botrychium multifidum
Adder's tongue family
(Ophioglossaceae)
Quick ID: leathery dissected triangular leaves; tiny green grape-like spores on separate stalk, 6–17.7"
Height: 1.2–13"

More primitive than true ferns, grape ferns belong to a group of plants called fern allies, which have an ancient lineage, first arriving in the fossil record over 350 million years ago. Grape ferns are named for the stalk of round, grape-like spores that are borne on a tall spike. Look for leathery grape fern near White Wolf.

INDIAN'S DREAM
Aspidotis densa
Maidenhair fern family
(Pteridaceae)
Quick ID: leathery, broadly triangular fronds with rolled margins; shiny brown stalks
Height: 2–11.8"

Indian's dream, or dense lace fern, is a wispy triangular fern on long stems that arise from a tuft of roots called rhizomes. Resembling a flattened grove of miniature trees, Indian's dream is similar in appearance to the American parsley fern (*Cryptogramma acrostichoides*) but only has one type of frond.

AMERICAN PARSLEY FERN
Cryptogramma acrostichoides
Maidenhair fern family (Pteridaceae)
Quick ID: stalks in clumps; sterile fronds look like parsley, fertile fronds with curled leaf blades
Height: 4–12"

American parsley fern is a rock lover often found on cliffs and rock faces. This lovely fern has two types of fronds—a lacy sterile frond that looks like parsley and a fertile frond that has somewhat straight to oval blades that curl over the spores.

GOLDBACK FERN
Pentagramma triangularis
Maidenhair fern family (Pteridaceae)
Quick ID: 5-lobed triangular fronds, golden yellow waxy spores on underside of frond; reddish stem
Height: 4–15"

Goldback fern is a native of western states from Arizona to Washington and into British Columbia. It often grows on slopes and along road banks where it can find a toehold in rock crevices. True to its name, if you look on the underside of this fern, it has golden spores. Look for this interesting fern in dry habitats near the Arch Rock Entrance, El Portal, Foresta, and Hetch Hetchy.

LADY FERN
Athyrium filix-femina
Cliff fern family (Woodsiaceae)
Quick ID: tufts or clumps of lacy fronds; frond broadest near middle, tapering at both ends
Height: 8–35"

With its lacy leaves and arching fronds, lady ferns form graceful bouquets in open thickets and moist woods. You can see lady fern in the subalpine and alpine regions in the park, including Tuolumne Meadows. Lady and wood fern (*Dryopteris arguta*) are the two large ferns that are seen in Yosemite Valley. The fronds of wood fern are not narrow at the base like those of lady fern.

FRAGILE FERN
Cystopteris fragilis
Cliff fern family (Woodsiaceae)
Quick ID: clustered fronds, broad lance-shaped; stalks reddish at base
Height: 4–12"

Found on streambanks and moist woods, fragile fern is well named, as the brittle fronds break easily when bent. As with most ferns, the tiny spores are found on the bottom of the frond in protective dots called sori, which comes from a Greek word meaning "pile" or "heap." The sorus opens when it dries, releasing the spores.

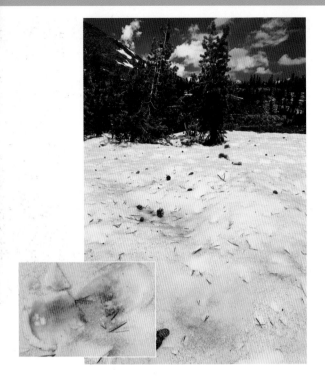

WATERMELON SNOW
Chlamydomonas nivalis
Green algae family (Chlamydomonadaceae)
Quick ID: streaks or patches of red-pink snow
Length: 0.00078–0.00118"

Spring visitors to the High Sierras sometimes find patches of melting snow that is pale red, not unlike the color of watermelon flesh. This phenomenon, called watermelon snow, is caused by microscopic green algae that thrive in freezing water. The origin of all land plants, green algae are members of an ancient family. These particular green algae contain carotenoid, a red pigment that helps protect it from the UV radiation at high altitudes. Consuming watermelon snow is not advised, as it can cause diarrhea.

TWISTED MOSS
Tortula ruralis
Pottia moss family (Pottiaceae)
Quick ID: thin, translucent recurved leaves with long hairlike tip

Mosses are very simple plants that absorb water and nutrients mainly though their leaves rather than roots. Like most mosses, twisted moss is less than an inch tall, but up close, it looks like a forest of tiny Lilliputian trees.

HANSEN'S SPIKEMOSS
Selaginella hansenii
Spikemoss family (Selaginellaceae)
Quick ID: stem with short overlapping spiral scale-like leaves

An ancient group of plants that grew on Earth 400 million years ago, spikemosses are not true mosses and not true ferns. They are sometimes referred to as "fern allies" but have characteristics closer to other primitive plants called club mosses and quillworts. Endemic to California, Hansen's spikemoss is found in Yosemite Valley and Hetch Hetchy growing in low, branched mats. When dry, Hansen's and some other spikemosses curl into tight, light brown fists and appear dead; but when it rains, they spring back to life. This capability has earned them the name "resurrection plant."

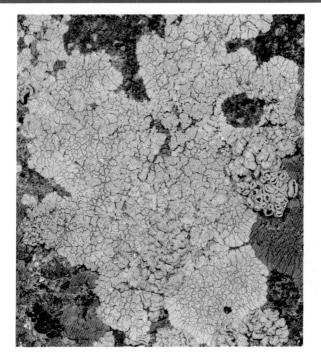

GOLD COBBLESTONE LICHEN
Pleopsidium flavum
Cobblestone and cracked lichen family (Acarosporaceae)
Quick ID: yellow segments on rock
Type: crustose (flat)

Cracked crust lichens such as the gold cobblestone lichen are separated into tiny segments that resemble cobblestones in an old road. Lichen is a mutualistic relationship between a fungus that provides shelter and an alga or cyanobacteria that photosynthesizes the sun's energy. Sharing resources, they can live in areas where neither could grow alone.

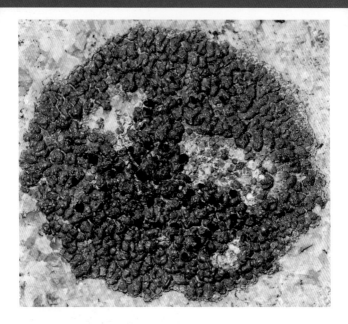

BROWN TILE LICHEN
Lecidea atrobrunnea
Disk and tile lichen family (Lecideaceae)
Quick ID: puffy reddish-brown "tiles" set on a black background
Type: crustose (flat)

There are several types of tile lichens, which look something like they were fit together like tiles on a walkway. Crustose lichens are flat and adhere tightly to their rock (or other) substrate. Due to their slow growth, some tile lichens are used to date geologic events.

TREE-HAIR LICHEN
Bryoria fremontii
Shield lichen family (Parmeliaceae)
Quick ID: thick hairlike twisted strands with thinner perpendicular side strands
Type: fruticose (shrubby)

Tree-hair lichen grows in long dense hairlike strands on conifers. It has long been used for food and for fibers for clothing. Lichens absorb dust and other particulate matter from the air to obtain nutrients; thus they are exposed to whatever is carried in the air. Tree-hair lichen is very sensitive to air pollution, and park biologists are studying these and other lichen populations in the park.

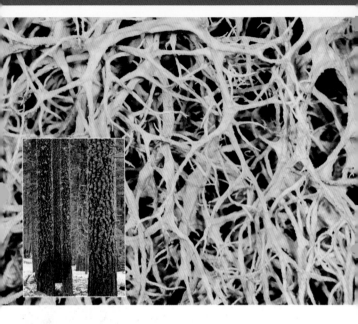

WOLF LICHEN
Letharia vulpina
Shield lichen family (Parmeliaceae)
Quick ID: bright greenish-yellow, thin branching strands
Type: fruticose (shrubby)

Poisonous beauties of the forest, long bright greenish-yellow strands of wolf lichen hang gracefully from conifer trunks and branches. This lichen contains the yellow pigment vulpinic acid and was an important source of yellow dye. Wolf lichen was once used in Europe to poison wolves and foxes. A reliable spot to look for wolf lichens are the conifer forests near Crane Flat.

BROAD WRINKLE LICHEN
Tuckermannopsis platyphylla
Shield lichen family (Parmeliaceae)
Quick ID: reddish-brown with yellowish-green, irregular wrinkled lobes; warty
Type: foliose (leafy)

Broad wrinkle lichen grows on bark and branches of trees, especially conifers. Lichens are categorized into three main types: fruticose, which are shrubby or bushy; crustose, which lie flat on rocks, trees, or other substrates; and foliose, which are leaflike.

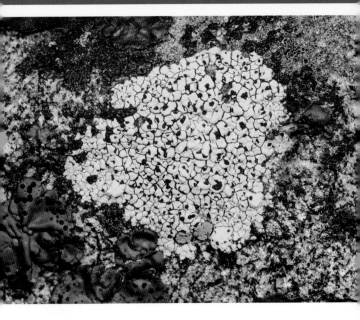

YELLOW MAP LICHEN
Rhizocarpon geographicum
Map lichen family (Rhizocarpaceae)
Quick ID: yellow tiles, black central dot
Type: crustose (flat)

Pieced together like a stone walkway, the yellow map lichen grows very slowly. At a growth rate of about 0.44 inch per century, map lichens are used to determine the age of geologic events, such as glacial retreat.

ELEGANT SUNBURST LICHEN
Xanthoria elegans
Sunburst lichen family (Teloschistaceae)
Quick ID: bright orange patches on rock
Type: crustose (flat)

Colorful sunburst lichens often grow in the vicinity of pika dens or bird roosts, as they grow best in well-fertilized, nutrient-rich environments.

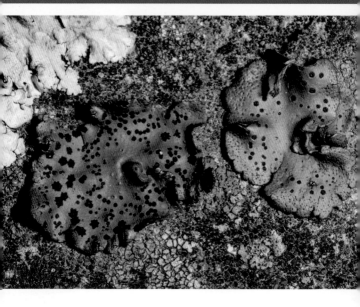

EMERY ROCK TRIPE
Umbilicaria phaea
Umbilicate family (Umbilicariaceae)
Quick ID: brown with black square or star-shaped marks, flat circular with tattered edges, bumpy black underneath; attached to rocks
Type: foliose (leafy)

Found at elevations below 8,000 feet on dry, exposed rocky areas, emery rock tripe is one of the most widespread lichens in the western states. The black, rough underside led to the common name emery, as it resembles an emery board used for filing fingernails. Rock tripe grows from a central "stalk" that is attached to the surface of a rock.

SIERRA SCULPTURED PUFFBALL
Calvatia sculpta
Agaricus family (Agaricaceae)
Quick ID: baseball-size; round white with pyramid-shaped warts and bent pointed tips

Typical puffball mushrooms are rounded with smooth or rough "skin" and come in many sizes from marble size to some the size of a basketball. Sporting pyramid-shaped warts and bent tips, the Sierra sculptured puffball is one of the most distinctive of all mushrooms. As with many puffballs, these are edible and are often cooked in a puffball lasagna dish.

AMANITA COCCORA
Amanita calyptroderma
Amanita family (Amanitaceae)
Quick ID: golden brown cap with white patch; gills whitish; white stalk, veil on stalk, volva at base

Many members of the Amanita family are poisonous—some even deadly. While amanita coccora is not poisonous, it may be easily confused with some of its lethal relatives. Most amanitas fruit up from the ground covered by a white membrane called a universal veil, which often remains stuck in patches on the cap. Some like coccora have a skirt-like ring on the stem and a saclike structure called a volva at the base. The fly agaric, *A. muscaria* (inset), has a ringlike volva.

SPRING KING BOLETE
Boletus rex-veris
Bolete family (Boletaceae)
Quick ID: large and robust; reddish-brown cap; stalk with netlike markings; pores yellowish-white to olive-yellow; does not bruise blue

King boletes are delicious edibles, and these large mushrooms are enjoyed by many people. Boletes do not have gills like many other mushrooms. Instead, if you look under the cap, they have pores from which the spores are released.

WOOLLY CHANTERELLE
Turbinellus floccosus
Gomphoid family (Gomphaceae)
Quick ID: dull orange, bruising brownish; vase-shaped with deep central depression; buffy underneath with wrinkled folds

A mushroom in disguise, the woolly or scaly vase chanterelle is not a chanterelle at all. Unlike many delicious chanterelles, eating this mushroom may make you quite sick. It has long been placed in the genus *Gomphus* but was recently moved to the genus *Turbinellus*.

OYSTER MUSHROOM
Pleurotus ostreatus
Pleurotus family (Pleurotaceae)
Quick ID: white shelflike clusters on dead standing trees or fallen logs; gills underneath; top turns tan in winter

Mycophiles (mushroom lovers) find fall a great time to search for the edible oyster mushroom, which often forms large shelflike masses on fallen trees. Highly nutritious, oyster mushrooms are high in selenium, potassium, and B vitamins and may help lower cholesterol levels due to a compound called lovastatin.

CRYPTIC GLOBE FUNGUS
Cryptoporus volvatus
Polypore family (Polyporaceae)
Quick ID: white to brown polypore, looks like a puffball or glob of chewing gum on wood; veil covers pores

Sometimes called veiled polypore, the cryptic globe fungus depends on wood-boring beetles to carry its spores to other wood.

PINKISH CORAL FUNGUS
Ramaria formosa
Coral fungi family (Ramariaceae)
Quick ID: coral-like, branching; yellowish-pink

Seeming more suited for a life under the ocean than a terrestrial existence, the pinkish coral fungus has the appearance of a sea urchin or coral. Coral fungi come in an assortment of lovely colors, from yellow or white to pink or even violet.

BROWN FELT BLIGHT
Neopeckia coulteri
Family not currently assigned
Quick ID: blackish-brown matted needles on pines

Deep under many feet of snow, a fungus called brown felt blight can infect pines when temperatures are mild enough. The fungus leaves the needles matted together and dead on the tree.

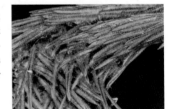

WILLOW ROSETTE GALL MIDGE
Rabdophaga salicisbrassicoides
Gall midge family (Cecidomyiidae)
Quick ID: green and red cabbage-like rosettes; resemble dried brown cones as they age

Galls can look like bumps, lumps, stars, balls, or cones. Generally they do not harm the plant. The gall that forms from the willow rosette gall midge resembles a cabbage-like cluster of leaves on willows. Midges are small flies, not all of which form galls.

HAIRY GALL WASP
Andricus lasius
Gall wasp family (Cynipidae)
Quick ID: round; look like fuzzy pinkish-tan cotton balls

Small wasps called cynipid wasps form these bizarre galls, which look like fuzzy pink or tan cotton balls, on the veins of canyon live oak leaves.

OAK PAPER GALL
Trichoteras vaccinifoliae
Gall wasp family (Cynipidae)
Quick ID: round, golf ball–size; thin, fleshy, mostly hollow inside; pale green turning papery brown

One of the most noticeable galls, the oak paper gall is a round gall on canyon live and huckleberry oaks caused by a cynipid wasp. When the wasp lays its eggs in the tree, the tissue reacts, creating a chamber or shell in which the wasp larvae grow and mature.

ROSY RED WILLOW GALL
Pontania sp.
Sawfly family (Tenthredinidae)
Quick ID: red bumps on willow leaves

Many gall insects are very specific to the plants on which they form galls, as well as which part of the plant they use. Sawflies are small wasps that have sawlike ovipositors (egg-laying organs). A gall begins to develop on willows when the female sawfly lays her eggs into the plant; the larvae grow here until they leave the gall. Other species form similar galls on manzanita.

GRANITE

Quick ID: various shades of gray, white, and black; coarse-grained with scattered dark minerals

Type: igneous rock

From immense cliffs and rounded domes to plunging waterfalls, granite is what gives Yosemite its majestic character. Formed millions of years ago from magma deep below the Earth's surface, granite is a white or grayish igneous rock with a "salt-and-pepper" appearance due to grains of white feldspars, gray quartz, and black biotites and hornblendes. Diorite contains lots of dark minerals; granodiorite has more dark minerals than diorite but less than granite. El Capitan granite is made up of quartz, plagioclase, orthoclase, and biotite. Half Dome granodiorite is characterized by black hornblende and biotite, smoky quartz, and white plagioclase and orthoclase.

References

Alden, P., F. Heath, A. Leventer, R. Keen, and W. B. Zomlefer. *National Audubon Society Field Guide to California.* New York: Alfred A. Knopf, Inc., Chanticleer Press, Inc., 1998.

Anderson, M. K. *Tending the Wild.* Berkeley and Los Angeles, CA: University of California Press, 2005.

Arora, D. *Mushrooms Demystified,* 2nd ed. Berkeley, CA: Ten Speed Press, 1986.

Baldwin, B. G., D. H. Goldman, D. J. Keil, R. Patterson, T. J. Rosatti, and D. H. Wilken, eds. *The Jepson Manual: Vascular Plants of California,* 2nd ed. Berkeley and Los Angeles, CA: University of California Press, 2012.

Blackwell, L. R. *Wildflowers of the Sierra Nevada and the Central Valley.* Renton, WA: Lone Pine Publishing, 1999.

Botti, S. J. *An Illustrated Flora of Yosemite National Park.* El Portal, CA: Yosemite Association, 2001.

Brinkley, E. S. *Field Guide to Birds of North America.* New York: Sterling Publishing Co., 2008.

Brock, J. P., and K. Kaufman. *Kaufman Field Guide to Butterflies of North America,* 2nd ed. New York: Houghton Mifflin, 2003.

Brodo, I. M., S. D. Sharnoff, and S. Sharnoff. *Lichens of North America.* New Haven, CT: Yale University Press, 2001.

Browning, P. *Yosemite Place Names,* 2nd ed. Lafayette, CA: Great West Books, 2005.

Clark, J. L., and R. W. Garrison. *Northern California Nature Weekends.* Guilford, CT: FalconGuides, 2005.

Cobb, B. *A Field Guide to Ferns and Their Related Families.* New York: Houghton Mifflin, 1984.

Crampton, B. *Grasses in California.* Berkeley and Los Angeles, CA: University of California Press, 1974.

Davis, R. M., R. Sommer, and J. A. Menge. *Field Guide to Mushrooms of Western North America.* Berkeley and Los Angeles, CA: University of California Press, 2012.

Dunkle, S. W. *Dragonflies through Binoculars: A Field Guide to Dragonflies of North America.* New York: Oxford University Press, 2000.

Durkee, D. J. *Easy Day Hikes in Yosemite.* El Portal, CA: Yosemite Association, 2000.

Eaton, R. E., and K. Kaufman. *Kaufman Field Guide to Insects of North America.* New York: Houghton Mifflin, 2007.

Eder, T. *Mammals of California.* Auburn, WA: Lone Pine Publishing, 2005.

Evans, A. V., and J. N. Hogue. *Field Guide to Beetles of California.* Berkeley and Los Angeles, CA: University of California Press, 2006.

Farmer, J. F. *Basketry Plants Used by Western American Indians.* Fullerton, CA: The Justin Farmer Foundation, 2010.

Forsyth, A. *Mammals of North America: Temperate and Arctic Regions.* Buffalo, NY: Firefly Books, 2006.

Glassberg, J. *Butterflies through Binoculars: The West.* New York: Oxford University Press, 2001.

Glazner, A. F., and G. M. Stock. *Geology Underfoot in Yosemite National Park.* Missoula, MT: Mountain Press Publishing Company, 2010.

Grater, R. K. *Discovering Sierra Mammals.* Yosemite Natural History Association and Sequoia Natural History Association, 1978.

Harris, A. G., E. Tuttle, and S. D. Tuttle. *Geology of National Parks,* 6th ed. Dubuque, IA: Kendall/Hunt Publishing, 2004.

Hartson, T. *Squirrels of the West.* Auburn, WA: Lone Pine Publishing, 1999.

Heizer, R. F., and A. B. Elsasser. *The Natural World of the California Indians.* Berkeley and Los Angeles, CA: University of California Press, 1980.

Hill, M. *Geology of the Sierra Nevada.* Berkeley and Los Angeles, CA: University of California Press, 2006.

Horn, E. L. *Sierra Nevada Wildflowers.* Missoula, MT: Mountain Press Publishing Co., 1998.

Jameson, E. W., and H. J. Peeters. *Mammals of California.* Berkeley and Los Angeles, CA: University of California Press, 2004.

Jepson Flora Project, eds. Jepson eFlora, 2013; 23 August 2013; ucjeps.berkeley .edu/IJM.html.

Johnston, V. R. *Sierra Nevada: The Naturalist's Companion.* Berkeley and Los Angeles, CA: University of California Press, 1998.

Kiver, E. P., and D. V. Harris. *Geology of U.S. Parklands,* 5th ed. New York: John Wiley & Sons, 1991.

Lanner, R. M. *Conifers of California.* Los Olivos, CA: Cachuma Press, 1999.

Laws, J. M. *The Laws Field Guide to the Sierra Nevada.* Berkeley, CA: Heyday Books, 2007.

Lightfoot, K. G. and O. Parrish. *California Indians and Their Environment.* Berkeley and Los Angeles, CA: University of California Press, 2009.

References

Lukas, D. *Sierra Nevada Birds*. Big Oak Flat, CA: Lukas Guides, 2011.

Medley, S. P. *The Complete Guidebook to Yosemite National Park,* 7th ed. Yosemite Conservancy, Berkeley, CA: Heyday Books, 2012.

Milne, L., and M. Milne. *The Audubon Society Field Guide to North American Insects and Spiders.* New York: Chanticleer Press, 1980.

Morgenson, D. C. *Yosemite Wildflower Trails.* El Portal, CA: Yosemite Association, 1975.

O'Neill, E. S. *Meadow in the Sky.* Groveland, CA: Albicaulis Press, 1993.

Ortiz, B. R. *It Will Live Forever.* Berkeley, CA: Heyday Books, 1991.

Page, L. M., and B. M. Burr. *Peterson Field Guide to Freshwater Fishes of North America North of Mexico,* 2nd ed. New York: Houghton Mifflin Harcourt Publishing Company, 2011.

Parisi, M., ed. *Atlas of the Biodiversity of California.* State of California, The Resources Agency, Department of Fish and Game, 2003.

Pavlik, B. M., P. C. Muick, S. G. Johnson, and M. Popper. *Oaks of California.* Olivos, CA: Cachuma Press, 1991.

Petrides, G. A. *A Field Guide to Trees and Shrubs,* 2nd ed. New York: Houghton Mifflin, 1986.

Powell, J. A., and C. L. Hogue. *California Insects.* Berkeley and Los Angeles, CA: University of California Press, 1979.

Roney, B. *The Road Guide to Yosemite.* Yosemite National Park: Yosemite Conservancy, 2013.

Russo, R. *Field Guide to Plant Galls of California and Other Western States.* Berkeley and Los Angeles, CA: University of California Press, 2006.

Schaffer, J. P. *Yosemite National Park: A Natural History Guide to Yosemite and Its Trails,* 4th ed. Berkeley, CA: Wilderness Press, 1999.

Sibley, D. A. *National Audubon Society: The Sibley Guide to Birds,* 1st ed. New York: Chanticleer Press, 2000.

Spencer, S. *Flowering Shrubs of Yosemite and the Sierra Nevada.* Yosemite, CA: Yosemite Association, Berkeley, CA: Heyday Books, 2009.

Storer, T. I., R. L. Usinger, and D. Lukas. *Sierra Nevada Natural History.* Berkeley and Los Angeles, CA: University of California Press, 2004.

Stuart, J. D., and J. O. Sawyer. *Trees and Shrubs of California.* Berkeley and Los Angeles, CA: University of California Press, 2001.

Swedo, S. *Best Easy Day Hikes Yosemite National Park.* Guilford, CT: FalconGuides, 2010.

_____. *Hiking Yosemite National Park.* Guilford, CT: Globe Pequot Press, 2011.

Wiese, K. *Sierra Nevada Wildflowers,* 2nd ed. Guilford, Ct: Morris Book Publishing, LLC.

Willard, D. *A Guide to the Sequoia Groves of California.* El Portal, CA: Yosemite Association, 2000.

Wilson, D. E., and S. Ruff, eds. *The Smithsonian Book of North American Mammals.* Washington, DC: Smithsonian Institution, 1999.

Wilson, L., J. Wilson, and J. Nicholas. *Wildflowers of Yosemite.* Mariposa, CA: Sierra Press, Inc., 2005.

Yosemite: A Guide to Yosemite National Park. Washington, DC: Division of Publications, National Park Service, US Department of the Interior, 1989.

Glossary

alkaloid: bitter compound produced by plants to discourage predators

alternate leaves: growing singly on a stem without an opposite leaf

anther: tip of a flower's stamen that produces pollen grains

bract: modified leaf

branchlet: small branch

cache: storage area of food

capsule: a dry fruit that releases seeds through splits or holes

carrion: remains of a deceased animal

catkin: a spike, either upright or drooping, of tiny flowers

cubic foot: the volume of a cube with sides of 1 foot (0.3048 m) in length

deciduous: a tree that seasonally loses its leaves

diurnal: active by day

drupe: outer fleshy fruit, usually having a single hard pit that encloses a seed

ecosystem: a biological environment consisting of all the living organisms in a particular area, as well as the nonliving components such as water, soil, air, and sunlight

endemic: growing only in a specific region or habitat

ethnobotany: the study of the relationship between plants and people

evergreen: a tree that keeps its leaves (often needles) year-round

genus: taxonomic rank below family and above species; always capitalized and italicized

glean: to pick small insects from foliage

habitat: the area or environment where an organism lives or occurs

host: an organism that harbors another organism

introduced: a species living outside its native range; often introduced by human activity

krummholz: stunted trees at high-altitude timberline

leaflet: a part of a compound leaf; may resemble an entire leaf but is borne on a vein of a leaf rather than the stem. Leaflets are referred to as pinnae; compound leaves are pinnate (featherlike).

migration: movement of birds and animals between breeding grounds and wintering areas

native: a species indigenous or endemic to an area

nectar: sweet liquid produced by flowers to attract pollinators

niche: an organism's response to available resources and competitors (like a human's job)

nocturnal: active at night

omnivore: feeding on a variety of foods, including both plant and animal materials

opposite leaves: growing in pairs along the stem

pollen: small powdery particles that contain a plant's male sex cells

pollination: transfer of pollen from an anther (male) to a stigma (female)

pome: a type of fruit consisting of an outer fleshy portion enclosing seeds in a tough central core

proboscis: elongated tubular insect mouthpart used for feeding and sucking

resin: a sticky substance formed from plant secretions

rhizome: underground stem that grows horizontally and sends up shoots

samara: papery winged seed

sepal: usually green leaflike structures found underneath the flower

species: taxonomic rank below genus (always italicized but never capitalized); also called "specific epithet"

stamen: male part of the flower composed of a filament, or stalk, and an anther, the sac at the tip of the filament that produces pollen

taxonomy: study of scientific classifications

tepal: a term used when petals and sepals have similar appearance

toothed: jagged or serrated edge

tufa: limestone formations formed by the precipitation of carbonate minerals in an alkaline lake

wing bar: line of contrastingly colored plumage formed by the tips of the flight feathers of birds

winged: thin, flattened expansion on the sides of a plant part

Index

Index

Index

About the Authors

Professional photographers, biologists, authors, and noted national park experts, Ann and Rob Simpson have spent years involved with research and interpretation in US national parks. They have written numerous books on national parks coast to coast that promote wise and proper use of natural habitats and environmental stewardship. As a former chief of interpretation and national park board member, Rob has a unique understanding of the inner workings of the national park system. In cooperation with American Park Network, both have led Canon "Photography in the Parks" workshops in major national parks, including Yosemite, Yellowstone, Grand Canyon, and Great Smoky Mountains.

Ann and Rob are both award-winning biology professors at Lord Fairfax Community College in Middletown, Virginia. With a background in science education, Ann heads the science department. As part of the college's nature photography curriculum, the Simpsons regularly lead international photo tours to parks and natural history destinations around the world.

Long known for their stunning images of the natural world, their work has been widely published in magazines such as *National Geographic, Time, National Wildlife,* and *Ranger Rick,* as well as many calendars, postcards, and books. You can see their work at Simpson's Nature Photography: www.agpix.com/snphotos.